Learn Stock trading From scratch

Preface

In this book, I put all of the information about the stock market from basic to advanced levels. My intention is to write this book just for educating people about the stock market that how easy this market is

I tried to make you understand everything in short words. I wrote chapters in few lines and simple words, So the readers can understand each and every topic in just few words and in an easy way.

Most of the people think that this market is quite complicated but this is not true. I put my all knowledge about the stock trading in a quite easy way. This book is not hard to understand.

So, This is all about this book. Read this book thoroughly and understand the stock trading in an easy way.

CONTENTS

Risk management and money management

The basics things about the market

1:) What is the stock market?

Share market, stock market and equity market the definition of these words are the same. You can say whatever you want. So, what is the share market? Share which means we are sharing something with someone else. Share means partnership. So, if you are buying the share of a particular company then it means you are buying a partnership of a particular company.

Now, you bought the shares of a company which means you have become a partner of that particular company. If a company will make a profit then you will also have that profit and if the company will make a loss then you will also have to bear that loss.

So, if a company needs financing or money then it has two options.

1. Debt financing
2. Equity financing

1. Debt financing:- Debt financing means the company have to take a loan or borrow money from somewhere else.

2. Equity financing:- Equity financing means the company can distribute their shares which means the company can distribute some part of their company to investors and can take money from investors.

If we talk about the history of the stock market then it is about 400 - 500 hundred years ago. Where a company whose name is dutch east India company exists. Nowadays it is related to the Netherlands.

At that time people have to invest money in ships if a ship goes to another country and does business and the ship will come back to the country then investors will have the profit from their investment.

So, the Dutch East India Company was the first company which was listed on the stock exchange.
So, Now the question has come: what is the stock exchange?

So, The stock exchange is a place where we can exchange our money into shares. Like, we go to the cloth shop and we buy cloth then we give the money to the shopkeeper. So, what is that? This is called an exchange. This means we have exchanged our money for cloth. Similarly, this is a stock exchange where we can exchange our money for shares.

So, the first stock exchange was built in the capital of the Netherlands Amsterdam. Its name is Amsterdam Stock Exchange and this was the first stock exchange in the world.

Nowadays, every country has their stock exchange.

And, the Share market contributes to a country's GDP and economic growth.

2:) What are sensex and nifty?

You might have heard about sensex, nifty 50, NASDAQ, dow jones, S&P 500 and etc. So, what are these?
These are called indices. Indices are a measurement of the price performance of a group of shares from an exchange. So, every stock exchange has its index. And these represent the overall situation of the market.

India has two major stock exchanges. The first one is BSE which means Bombay Stock Exchange and the second one is NSE which means National Stock Exchange.
BSE was established in 1875 and NSE was established in 1992. Both are situated in Mumbai.

Sensex is the index of BSE and nifty 50 is the index of NSE. Sensex represents the performance of the top 30 well-established and fundamentally strong companies. So, The top 30 companies of BSE are included in sensex. Similarly, The Nifty 50 represents the performance of the top 50 well-established and fundamentally strong companies.

Similarly, Every stock exchange has its index. Like, Tokyo stock exchange has Nikkei and New York Stock Exchange has NYSE Composite. So, These are the indices.

So, These indices can show the overall situation of the market. All you have to do just visit google and search there index name. Like, sensex, nifty, NASDAQ and etc

Now, I am going to show you a picture.

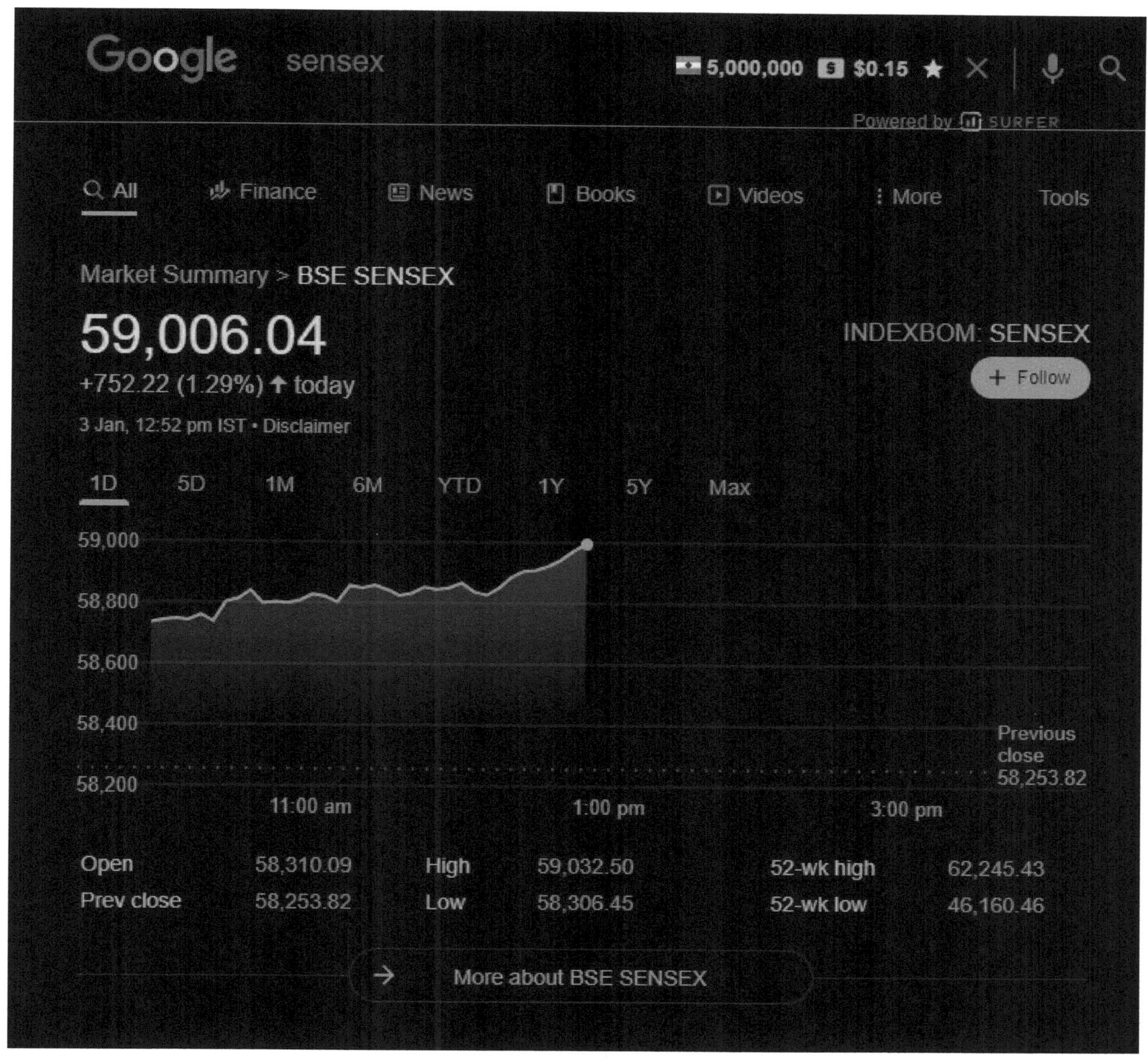

Here, I searched sensex and here you can see what is the situation of the market and where the market is going?

3:) What are demat and trading accounts?

Demat account is the thing where we can store our shares and the trading account is the thing where we can trade.

I want to explain to you with an example.

For example:- You went to the cloth shop and you bought some clothes then you paid money to the shopkeeper and the shopkeeper gave you clothes So, this is called trading and you have a purse and in that purse you have money. your money is stored in your purse. Now, your purse is working like a demat account.

The full name of the demat account is the Dematerialisation account. And it had been introduced in 1995. Before that people used to have share certificates.

Nowadays, the broker provides demat and trading accounts together.

4:) Who is the broker?

A broker works as a mediator between the stock exchange and a trader and investor.
Let me explain to you. There are three types of brokers.

1. Full-service broker
2. Bank broker
3. Discount broker

1:) Bank broker:- In the bank broker we have HDFC securities, ICICI securities, Kotak securities and etc.

A bank broker provides three in one account which means they open your trading account, Demat account and savings account. So, This is not the major reason that we should open our account with them. We can open our Demat account with other types of brokers. like, we can open our account with a full-service broker and we can link our account to the bank.

And they charge high brokerages and as well as they do not have a good and user-friendly interface.

2:) Full-service broker:- In the full-service broker we have Motilal Oswal, Sharekhan, IIFL and etc.

A full-service broker provides a relationship manager, call & trade facility, and Research report. A relationship manager helps us to solve our problems. Call & trade facility means you can just call them and tell them which stock you want to buy or sell, They do it on your behalf. A research report means they have a team of experts who pick some stocks, analyse those stocks and they make a research report and they send those reports to every investor whose account is in their brokerage firm. But they have high brokerages too.

3:) Discount broker:- In the discount broker we have Zerodha, Upstox, 5 paisa and etc.

A discount broker does not provide a relationship manager and a research report and they charge for call & trade facilities because of these they save much money. And they do not charge anything for delivery. Delivery means if you hold shares for more than a day then those will be included in the delivery. Discount brokers do not charge for delivery. They charge only for intraday. Intraday means you can buy and sell a charge in a day. After one day this will not be called intraday, this will be called delivery.

And they have a clean & beautiful user interface. I have been using a discount broker. And I suggest to you that you should go with them.

5:) What is SEBI?

SEBI Stands for Securities and Exchange Board of India. SEBI is like a security guard of the stock market. Like, RBI regulates rupees. Similarly, SEBI regulates the stock market.

SEBI is located in Mumbai. SEBI has the tremendous power to prohibit fraudulent trade activities associated with the securities market.

Every company has to get approved by SEBI before launching its IPO. SEBI has a responsibility that SEBI takes care of investors, and stop fraudulent activities.

SEBI was established in 1992 before SEBI controller of capital issues was the regulatory authority before SEBI came into existence.

6:) What is short selling?

Short selling is a method of trading. In this method when the market goes down we make money.

When a trader feels that a stock price will go down then he shorts that stock. He will use the method of short selling.

For example, Let's assume a stock whose name is 'XYZ' and the price of 'XYZ' is ₹500. A trader thinks that the 'XYZ' stock price will fall then he shorts stock of 'XYZ' and as he predicted that the price will go down as happened price went down and now the price is ₹450 and then he took an exit from that trade. So, he made ₹50 profit per share in this trade and this is how short selling works.

But, here's the problem that you can do short selling only for a day. You can do this only for intraday trading. If you want to do short selling for more than a day then you will have to do that in futures trading. We will discuss about future trading in futures trading's chapter.

7:) What is leverage?

Leverage means a broker lends you money and with that money you will trade in the stock market.

In leverage the share price of a share will be reduced.

For example, You have ₹5000 in your trading account and the share price of HDFC Bank is ₹1000 then how many shares you can buy with this amount? Only 5. Yes, you can buy only 5 shares with this amount. And if the share price will rise up and it went to ₹1050 then how much money did we make?

Only ₹250.

But, what if you will get more money for buying shares?
We looked that we can buy only 5 shares in ₹5000. But, if we take leverage then we get shares in just ₹100 and the quantity of shares is now 50. Now the share price rises up then similarly, it goes to ₹1050 then how much money did we make?

₹2500.

Now, you could imagine how big part of leverage there is in trading.

But, You can take leverage only for intraday trading which means you can take leverage only for a day. You can't do that for more than a day with actual shares. You can do this in futures trading.

Let's see how you can do on Zerodha's website

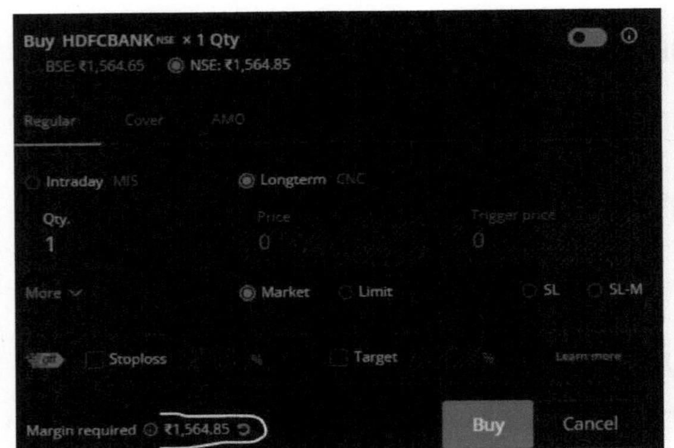

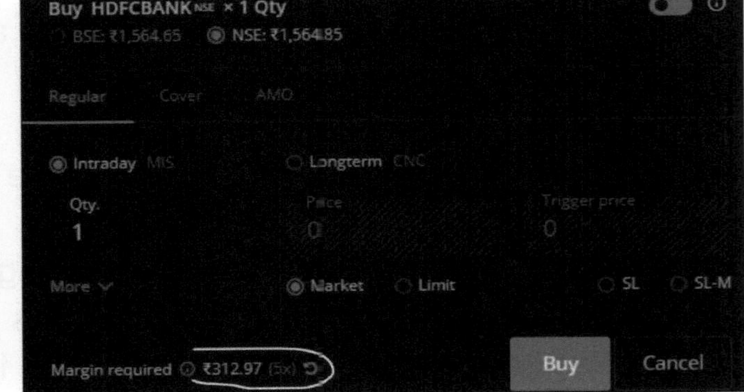

In this picture, we can see that when I selected long-term and below you can see the price is ₹1,564.85 and then I selected intraday here you can see the price has automatically been reduced. It is ₹312.97 and this is called leverage.

8:) How to buy and sell shares at Zerodha and Upstox?

We can easily buy and sell shares at Zerodha and Upstox easily. Now, I am going to show you everything step-by-step and make you understand with pictures.

First I am going to start with Zerodha.

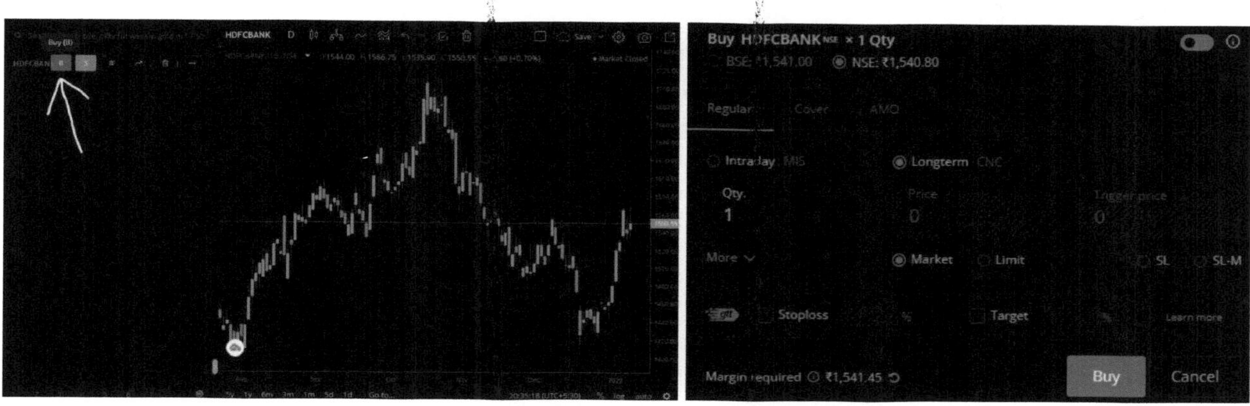

You can search for stock whichever you want to buy then click on buy. After clicking buy you can see this interface.

In this picture, we can see the upside that intraday and long-term.

Intraday:- You can see after intraday there is MIS which means Margin Intraday Square and intraday means you can buy and sell shares only for one day which means if you select intraday then if you buy and forget to sell your stock before the end of the trading session which is 3:30 PM IST then your stocks will automatically be sold.

Long-term:- You can see after long-term there is CNC which means Cash and Carry and long-term means if you buy stocks then you can sell whenever you want. It means you can hold more than a day which could be 2 days, 15 days,

1 month, 6 months, 1 year, 5 years or more than these means you can hold till whenever you want.

After this, you can see Qty.

Qty:- It means quantity. Here you can put the quantity of stocks that how many stocks you want to buy or sell.

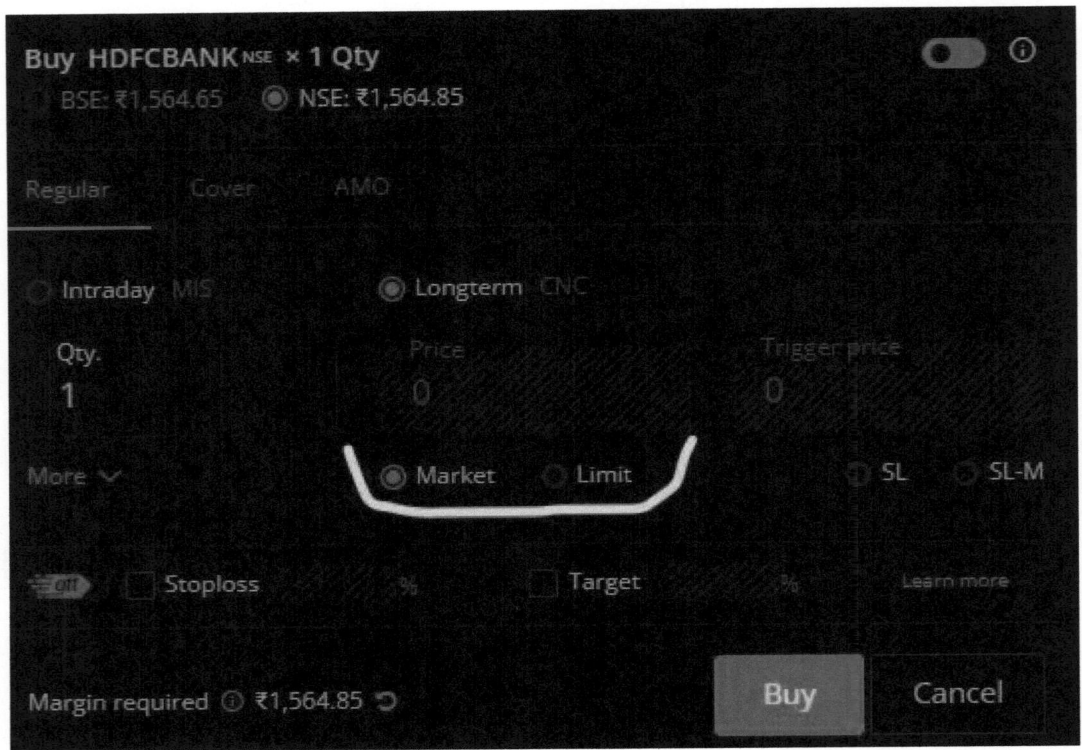

After Qty. you can see the market and limit order.

Market:- It means if you select market order then you have to buy at the market's price. For example:- In this picture, you can see that the price of HDFC Bank's share is ₹1,564.85 and this is the market's price and if you select market order and click on the buy option below this then your order will automatically be executed.

Limit:- It means you can customize the price. Let me show you how

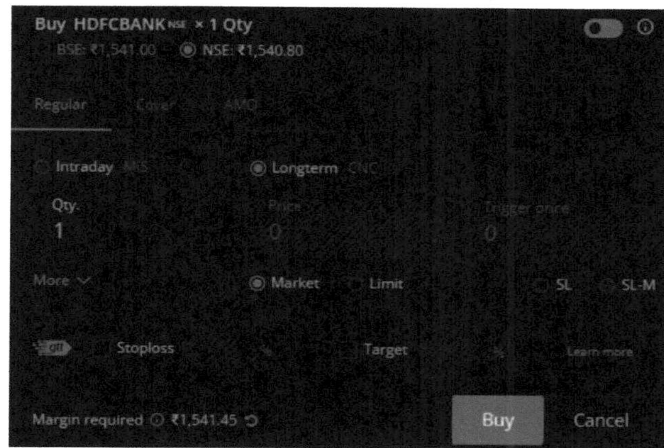

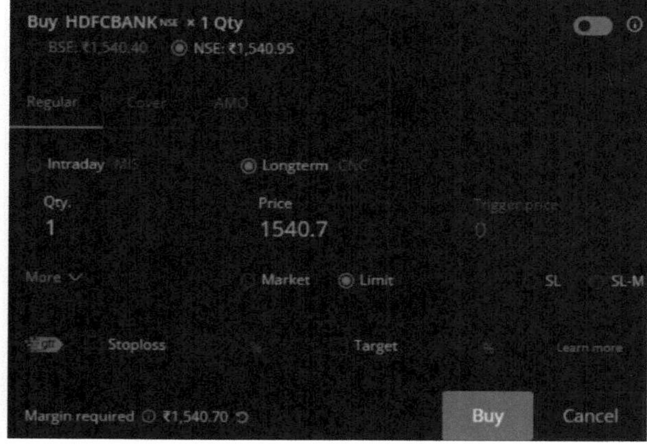

In this picture, you can see after selecting the limit order the price section which was blocked has now automatically been opened. Now, we can put a specific price here and if the market comes at that specific price then our order will automatically be executed. For example:- ‘XYZ’ is a stock and the price of this is ₹250 and we want to buy ‘XYZ’ when the price of stock comes at ₹220 then we can select the limit order and then put there ₹220 and if the stock price comes at ₹220 then our order will automatically be executed.

After the limit order, we can see SL and SL-M.

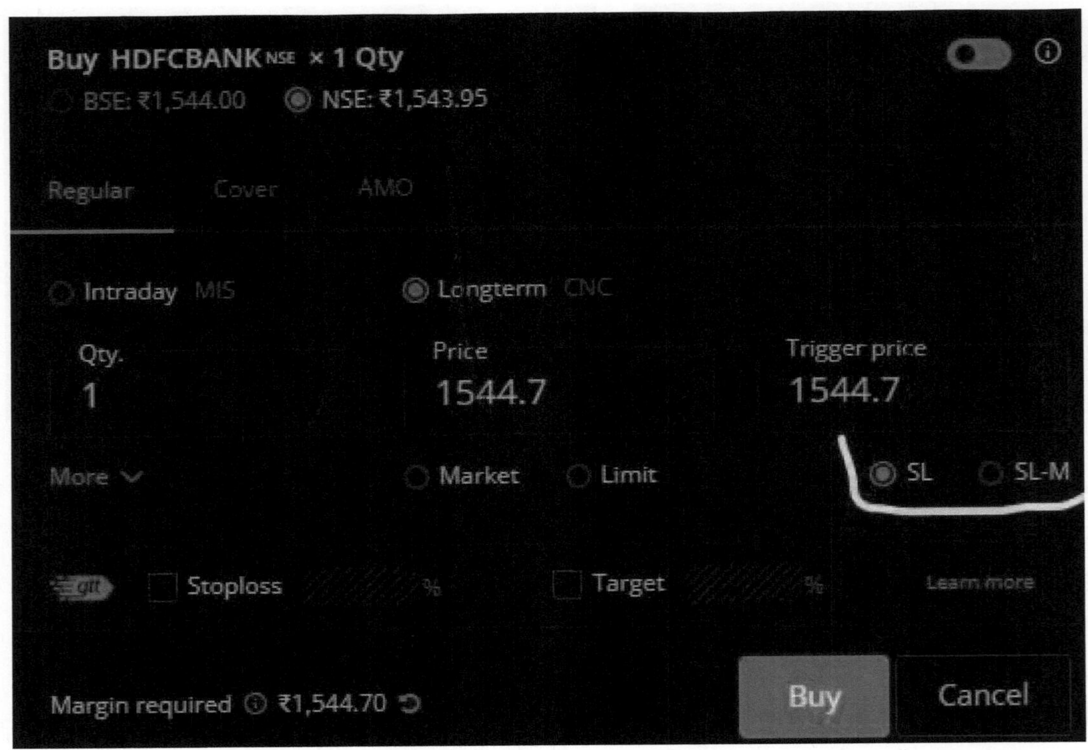

SL:- It means Stop Loss. SL word's definition is included in this word itself. We can limit our loss with the help of SL. After selecting SL order the price section and trigger price section have now been opened. Now, we can select a specific price as well as we can put the stop loss.

For example:- The price of 'XYZ' stock is ₹250 and we want to buy at ₹220, And then we put ₹200 in the trigger price section. In this case, if the share price comes at ₹220 then our order will be executed automatically. But unfortunately, if the share price goes down more and then hits our stop loss at ₹200 then our loss will be booked and if it goes down more then it won't affect us because our loss is limited. Let's assume it goes to ₹150 or ₹100 then it does not matter to us because our loss is limited.

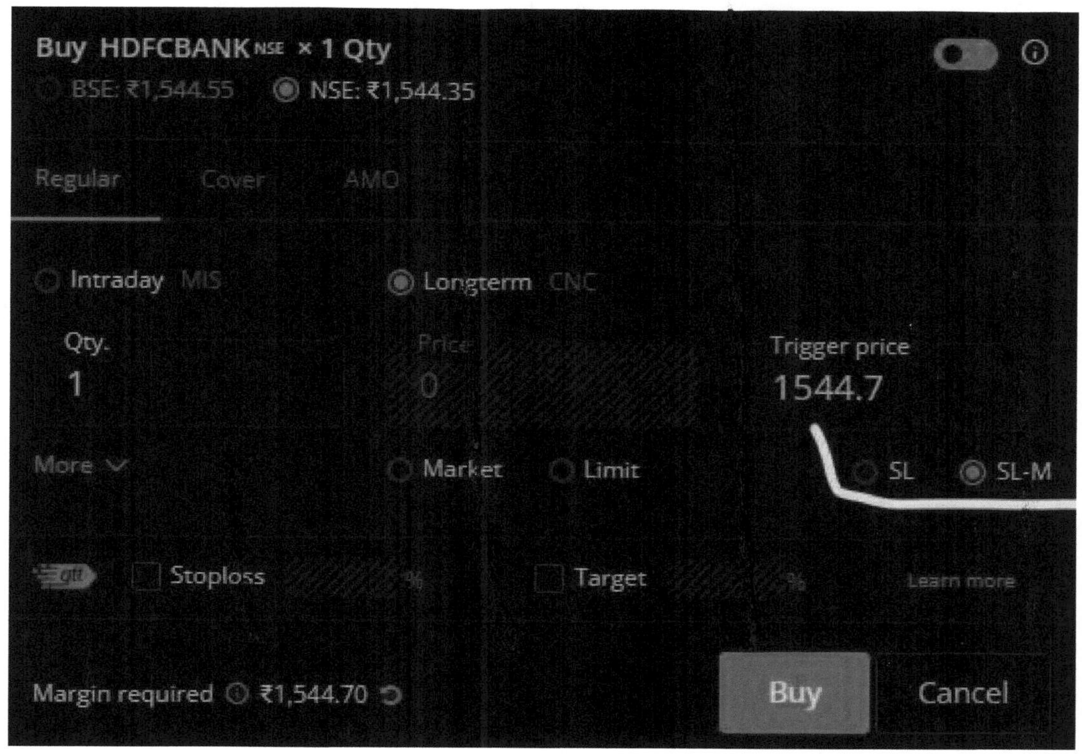

SL-M:- It means Stop Loss Market order. In this picture, you can see that the price section has been blocked. We now only can put trigger price. For example:- 'XYZ' stock's price is ₹250 and now we can buy at the market's price which is ₹250 and in the trigger price section we put ₹220. So, ₹220 is now our stop loss.

Below these order types, you can see GTT.

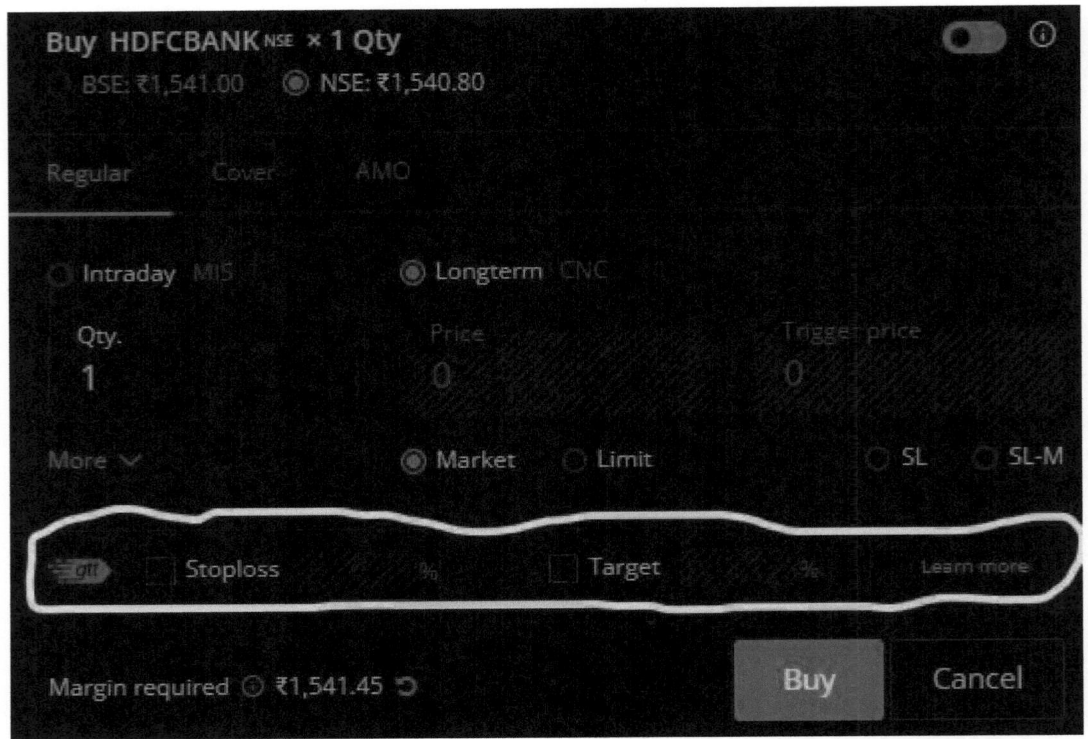

GTT:- It means Good Till Triggered. GTT is for long-term. We can select stop loss and target both things in gtt order.

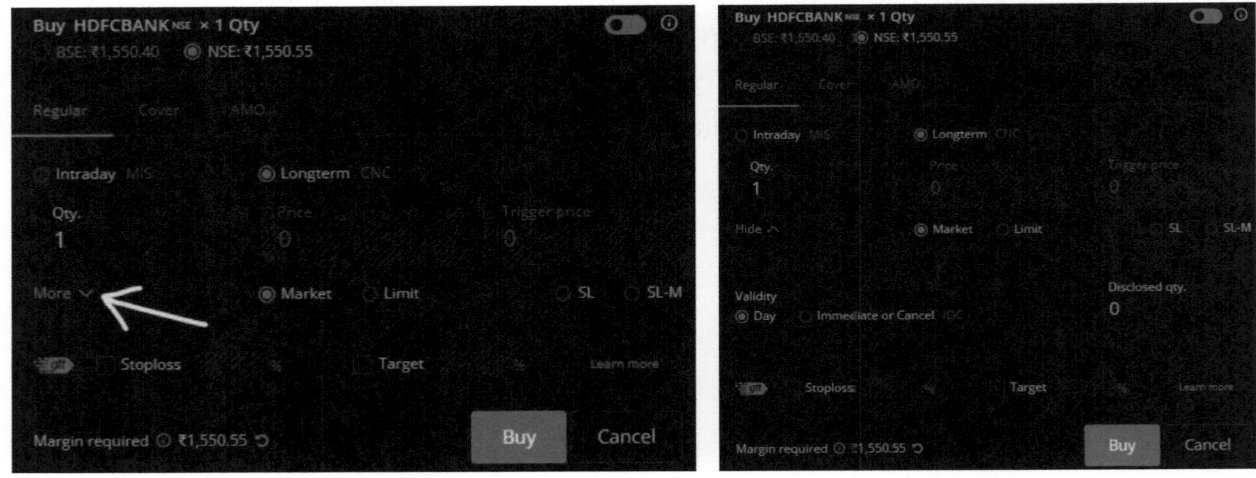

If we click at more as we can see in the picture then there are two options will open. The first one is validity and the second one is disclosed qty.

Validity:- In the validity there are two options day and IOC. Day order means If we buy a stock and our order didn't execute because that particular stock doesn't have too many buyers and sellers. This is called liquidity. In this case, if we select a day order then our order will be executed in an entire trading day and if that doesn't execute then our order will cancel.

IOC means Immediate or Cancel. If we buy a stock and if our order executes immediately then the stock will be bought and if the order doesn't execute at the moment then it will be cancelled.

Disclosed quantity:- It means we put a quantity here to disclose our order quantity to the market. It is an optional thing that you don't think about this thing too much.

Here on the upside, you can see three types of orders. The first one is regular, the second one is cover and the third one is AMO.

Here we have understood what is included in regular order. Now, we will see the cover order and AMO order.

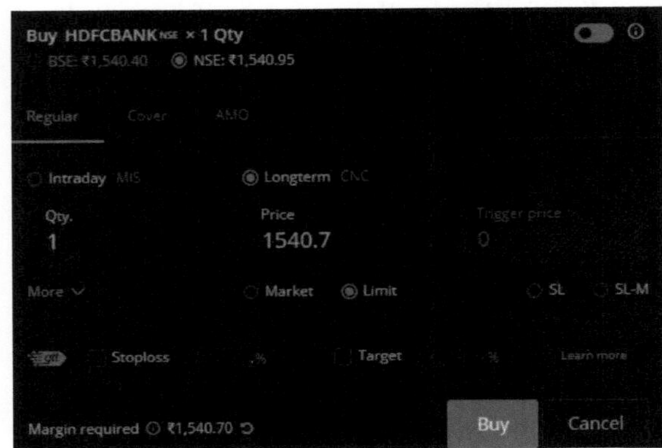

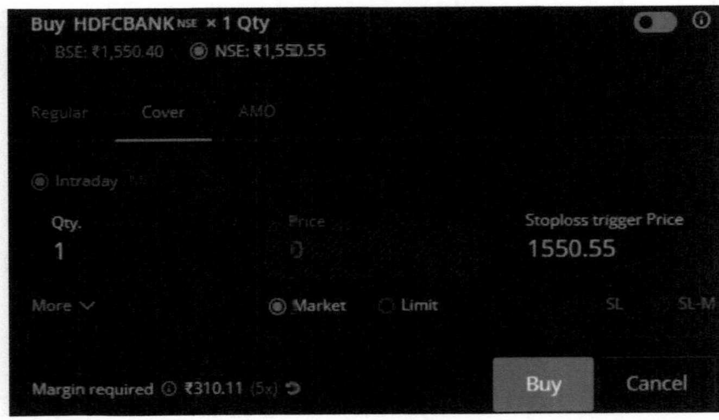

Cover order:- Cover is for intraday trading means it is for one day. And in cover order, you clearly can see that the long-term has been blocked. So, it is only used for one day. In cover order we can put quantity then in the stop loss trigger price section we can put stop loss. But we can modify the stop loss as well.
For example:- If a stock price is ₹500 and we bought at this price and put stop loss at 490 or 480 and if the stock price goes up then we can modify our stop loss too.

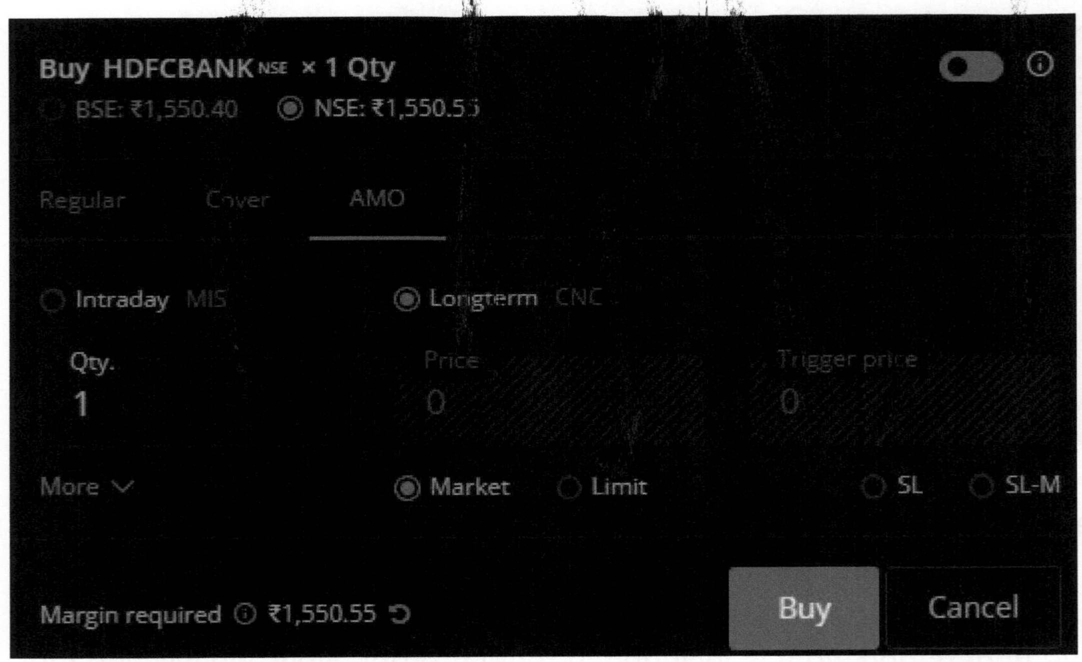

AMO:- It means After Market Order. The definition of this word is included in itself. It is used when the market is closed and we put our order for the next trading session. The Indian stock market opens at 9:15 AM IST and it closes at

3:30 PM IST and if we want to put our order after the market closes then we can choose an AMO order. You can use AMO order for intraday and long-term as you can see in the picture.

Now, We will see how to buy and sell shares at Upstox

So, there is not much difference between Zerodha and Upstox because the procedure is almost the same, only the interface is different.

For searching stock you just have to click on the upside plus(+) icon and then search for any stock whichever you want to buy.

After that click on buy then this interface will open you can see it in the picture on the right side. There are quantity, product, order type, complexity, disclosed quantity and validity.

In the quantity section, you have to put the quantity that how many stocks you want to buy.

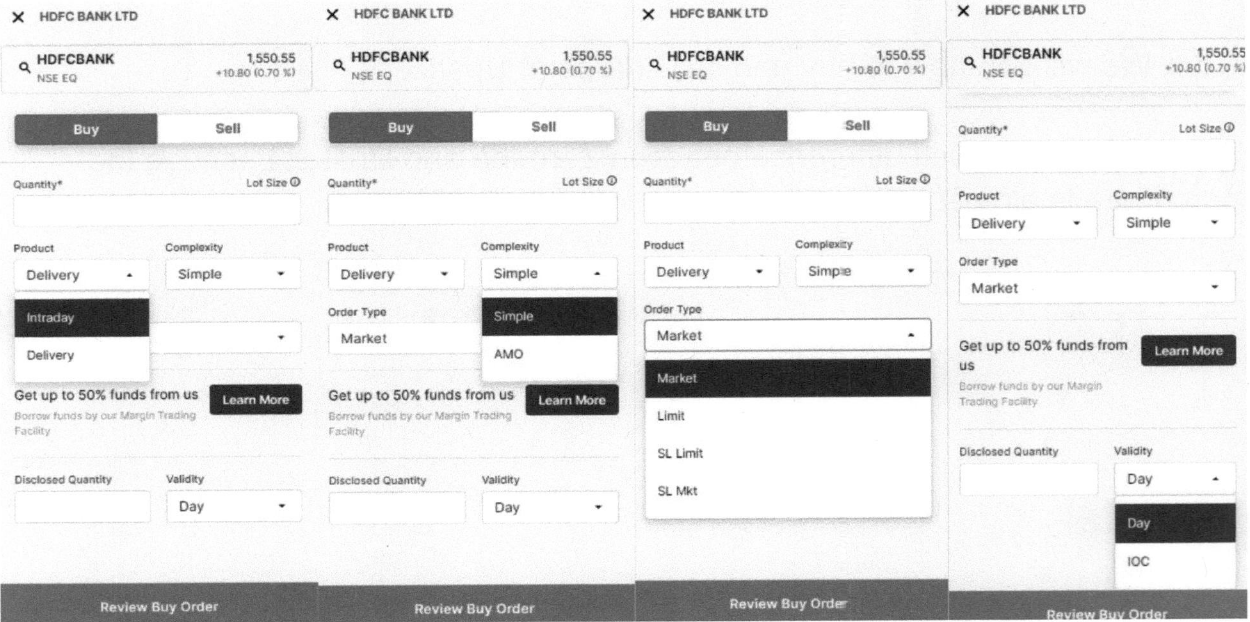

Product type:- In the product type we can see delivery and intraday. Delivery means we hold the stock for more than a day. If a stock is held for more than one day then it is included in the delivery. And the other name of delivery is long-term.

And the intraday means we can buy or sell a stock for a day as we have read before.

Now, The next one is complexity.

Complexity:- In complexity, we can see simple and AMO. Simple means we can put our order in the live market and AMO means we can put our order after the live market.

Order type:- In order type here we can see the market, limit, SL limit and SL market. Market means we can buy or sell at the market's price. Limit means we can decide our price like the stock price is ₹550 and we want to at ₹520 then we can do this in limit price.

SL limit means we can select our limit price as well as our stop loss. SL market means we can only choose the stop loss and we have to buy at the market's price.

Disclosed quantity:- A disclosed quantity is an optional thing and it allows investors and traders to disclose stock's quantity to the market.

Validity:- In the validity here we can see day and IOC. If we select day order and if we buy a stock then the order will be executed in the entire day means in an entire trading session. IOC means Immediate or Cancel which means if our order will be executed instantly then it will be cancelled.

So, this is how we can use Zerodha and Upstox.

9:) Types of trading

There are four types of trading.

1. Scalp trading
2. Intraday trading
3. Swing trading
4. Position trading

1. Scalp trading:- In scalp trading we hold shares from minutes to a few hours like we bought a share now and sell it after 30 minutes. This is called scalp trading.

2. Intraday trading:- this type of trading's definition is included in its name. Intraday means for one day like if we bought a share today morning then we will have to sell it before the trading session ends. In India, The market starts from 9:15 AM IST and closes at 3:30 PM IST. So, we have to sell it before 3:30 PM.

3. Swing trading:- In swing trading, we hold shares from a day to few days or few months like if we bought a share today then we can sell it after a week or after a month. We can hold shares until the target hits.

4. Position trading:- In position trading, we hold shares from a day to a few months. We hold them for 5 months, 8 months, 10 months and etc. So, if we buy shares for the long-term then this will be called position trading.

Futures and options trading

10:) What is futures trading?

Future trading is the part of derivatives. It is a contract and it has a validity period. The future contract expires last thursday of a month.

Now, I am going to make you understand with a picture.

In this picture you can see on the left side there is an actual stock of HDFC bank and after that, there are three future contracts. The first one is jan fut, the second one is feb fut and the third one is mar fut. So, when january month will end then a new future contract will be added which will be april future contract and as I said that every future contract expires on the last thursday of the month.

In the future contract, there are a lot sizes which are fixed. Let me show you.

In this picture, you can see the quantity of shares 550 which are fixed and this is called a lot. Every lot has different sizes. In this HDFC bank's future lot we can buy 550 shares in one lot. If we want to buy more shares then we have to put the quantity in the multiple of 550 which is 1100 shares. But we can't customize the quantity by ourselves like 2 shares, 100 shares etc.

So, let's talk about the advantages.

The first advantage of future trading is the required margin.

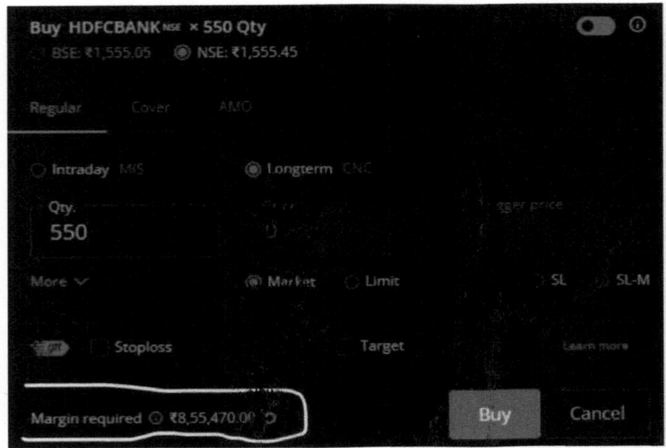

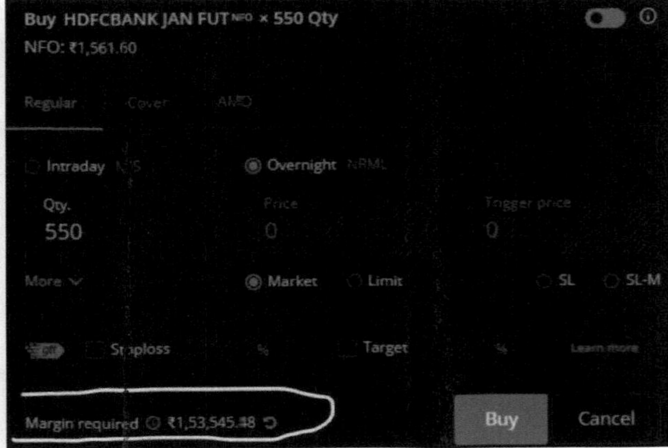

In this picture, You can clearly see the price difference. In the actual share of HDFC bank, we have to pay around 8 lakh rupees and the second one a future contract and in this contract, we have to pay around 1.5 lakh rupees. You can clearly see the difference. But we can hold future contracts for a limited time period.

The second advantage of future trading is short selling. We can't do short selling in actual shares for long-term but we can do this in future trading.

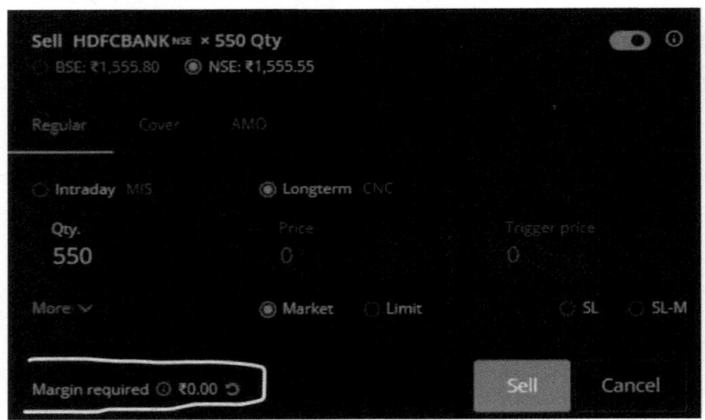

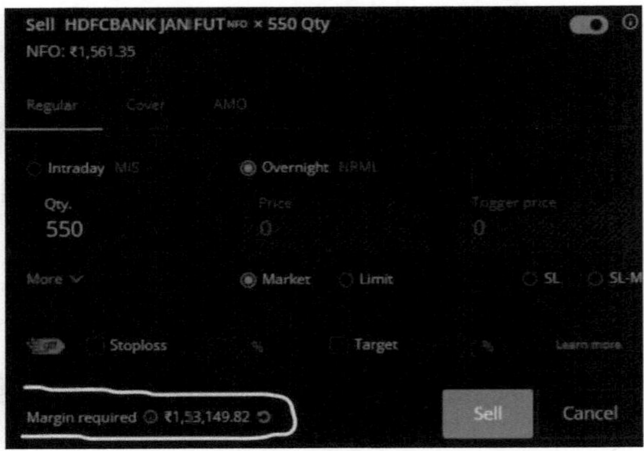

In this picture, We can see that in actual shares we can't do short sell but in future contracts we can. Yeah, this is for a limited period but we can do this for more than a day. This is the second advantage of future trading.

The third advantage of future trading is maximum profit.

As we have seen that we can buy 550 shares in one lot and let's assume the price goes up to 100 and in few weeks. So, How much did we make?

We've made 55,000 in just a few weeks. Yes, because it is not very high but we get too much profit.

But here is a problem: if you make a huge profit then you can also make losses too. But if you put stop loss, do trade with money management and manage your risk then it won't affect you.

11:) What is options trading?

Options trading is also the part of derivatives. Just as there is a contract in futures trading, there is also a contract in options trading. I am going to make you understand about options trading step by step.

Options trading has two sides CE and PE. CE means call option, It is used when the market goes up and PE means put option, It is used when the market goes down.

So, The definition of CE and PE are so simple. If the market goes up then we buy CE which means call option and if the market goes down then we buy PE which means put option.

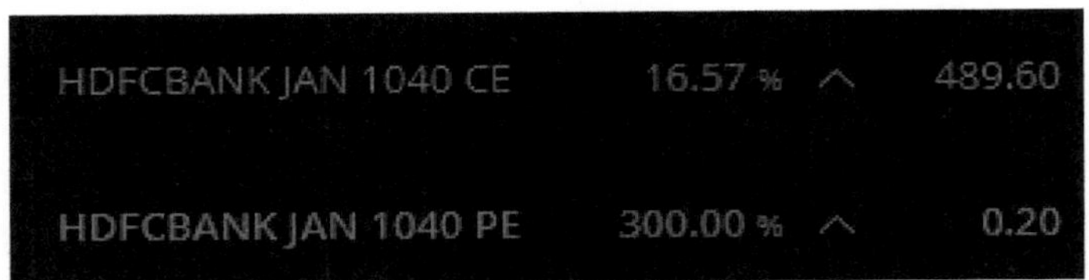

In this picture, you can see the CE option and PE option.

Did you notice one thing that I told you that buy PE when the market goes down? Because I am telling you about option buying, not option selling. Option buying is a different thing and option selling is a different thing.

So, What is option selling?
Option selling is the opposite of option buying as I told you that buy CE option when the market goes up but in option selling you have to sell the PE option when the market goes up. Read this again if you didn't understand.
Similarly, when the market goes down, sell the CE option.

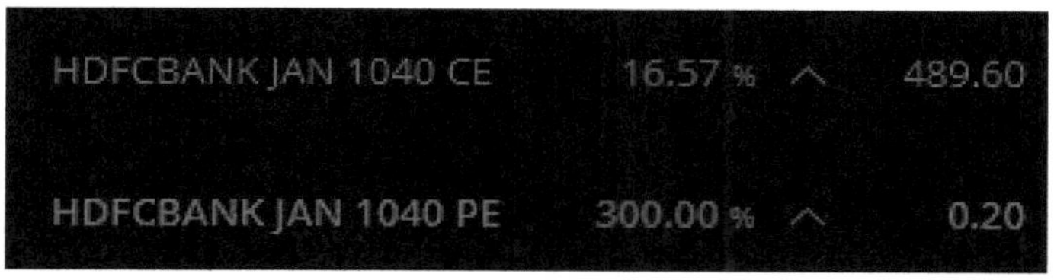

HDFCBANK JAN 1040 CE	16.57 % ^	489.60
HDFCBANK JAN 1040 PE	300.00 % ^	0.20

In this picture, you can see HDFCBANK JAN 1040 CE. SO, what is 1040? This is called the strike price.

In options trading, There are three types:- ITM, OTM and ATM.

ITM means In The Money, OTM means Out of The Money and ATM means At The Money.

Now, I am gonna make you understand. If I am telling something and that statement is true then it will be called ITM and if that statement is wrong then it will be called OTM.

Let's take an example:- We will write two options here like HDFCBANK JAN 1040 CE and HDFCBANK JAN 1640 CE. So, this is an option that we wrote here and let's assume we'll take the price of HDFCBANK's share is 1500.

HDFCBANK JAN 1040 CE
HDFCBANK JAN 1640 CE
HDFCBANK's share price = 1500

Now, I am giving a statement. The share price of HDFCBANK is more than the strike price which is 1040. I am telling here that the HDFCBANK's share price is more than 1040. Is this true?
Yes, This is true which means this is ITM. I told you earlier that if the statement is correct then it will be ITM.

Now, I am giving a statement of OTM. The HDFCBANK's share price will be more than the strike price and in this case, we're taking 1640. I am telling you again, The HDFCBANK's share price is more than 1640. Is this true?
No, This is not true. Because HDFCBANK's share price is not more than 1640, The share price is 1500. If the statement is not true then it will be OTM and in this case, this is OTM.

Now, What is an ATM?

ATM is used in future prediction like something is about to happen. I will make you understand with an example again.

HDFCBANK JAN 1040 CE
HDFCBANK JAN 1640 CE
HDFCBANK JAN 1510 CE
HDFCBANK's share price = 1500

I added here another option and the strike price of this option is 1510. I told you that if something is about to happen then this will be an ATM. HDFCBANK's share price is about to reach 1510. And this is about to reach at that level then it is ATM. ATM is not necessary but I explained it to you.

Well, We will see how this works in PE

The same definition is applied to it too, that is if something is true then it will be ITM and if it is wrong then it will be OTM. And something is about to happen then that will be an ATM.

HDFCBANK JAN 1640 PE
HDFCBANK JAN 1040 PE
HDFCBANK JAN 1490 PE
HDFCBANK's share price = 1500

I removed CE from here and wrote PE. PE means downside. So, I will make you understand one by one.

I am giving a statement. HDFCBANK's share price is less than 1640. Is this true? Yes, This is true because the share price of HDFCBANK is less than 1640.

Here is another statement. HDFCBANK's share price is less than 1040. Is this true? No, This is not true. Because the share price of HDFCBANK is not less than 1040.

Here's the statement of the ATM which is something that is about to happen. HDFCBANK's share price is about to reach 1490. Is this true? Yes, HDFCBANK's share price is about to reach 1490.

So, When do we take ITM and OTM?

If you think that the market will go a little bit up and after that it will be sideways and not much go up then you should go with ITM. We're talking about CE buying here.

But if you think that the market will have a strong up movement then you should go with OTM. But if you are a beginner then you should not go with OTM because it can destroy your capital.

Similarly, It happens in the PE option. If the market will go a little bit down and if it will be sideways then you should go with ITM and If you think the market will have a strong downside move then you should go with OTM.

Technical analysis

12:) What is the trend?

There are three types of trends. The first one is an uptrend, the second one is a downtrend and the third one is sideways.

Uptrend:- When the market goes up then this will be called an uptrend.

For example:-

Downtrend:- When the market goes down then this will be called a downtrend.

For example:-

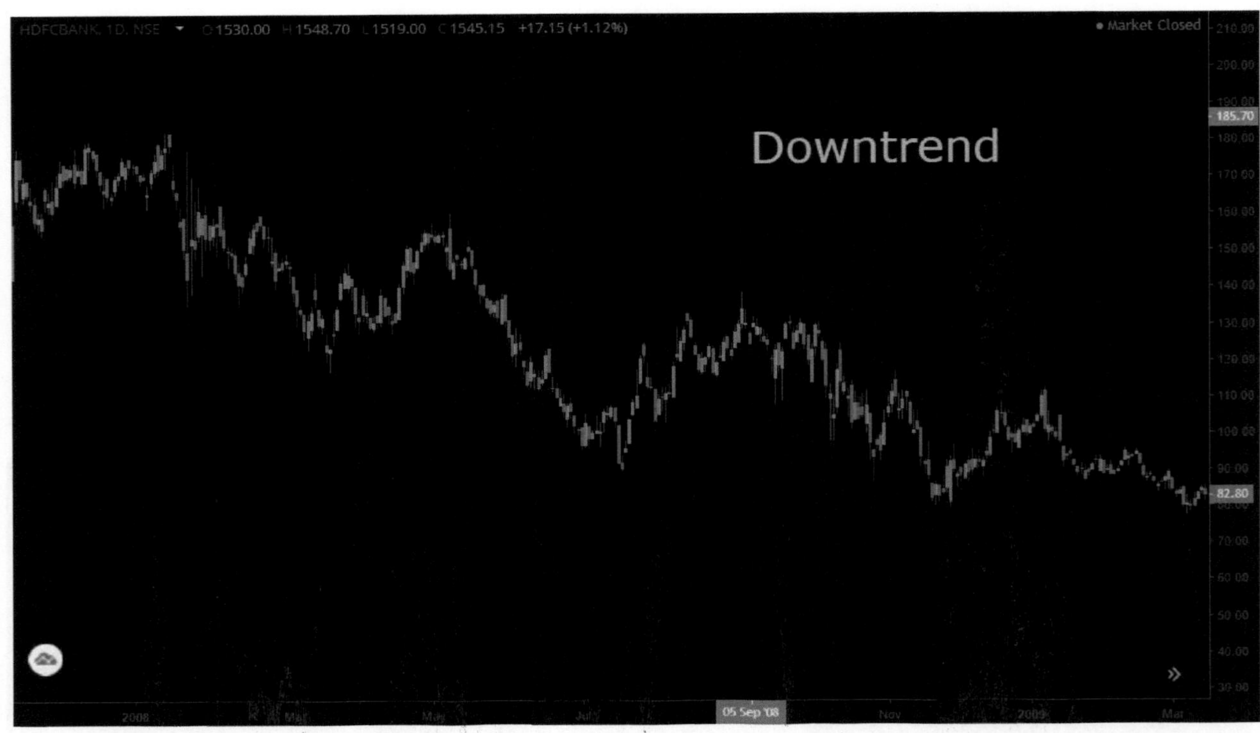

Sideways:- When the market goes in a range. The market goes down to up and up to down and roaming in a range then this will be called sideways. We can also say range-bound. Range-bound and sideways both are the same thing and we can say any of them.

For example:-

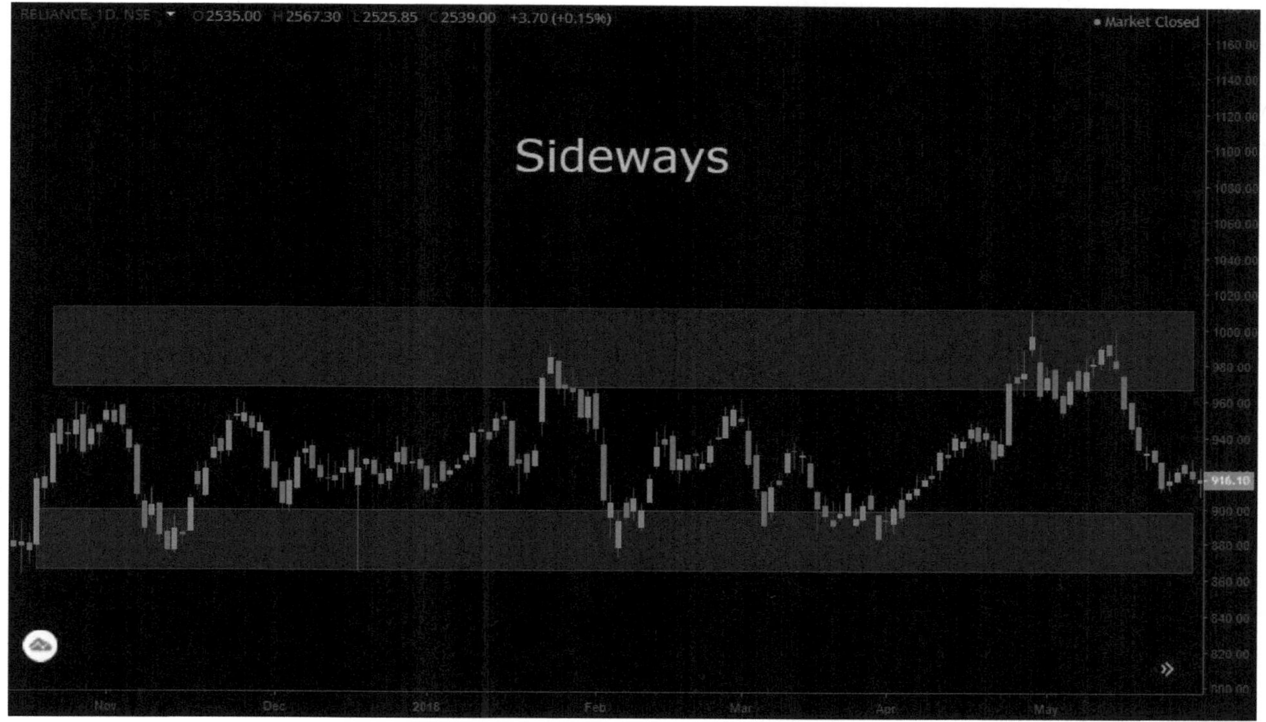

13:) Bullish candle and bearish candle

There are two types of candles in trading. The first one is a bullish candle and the second one is a bearish candle.

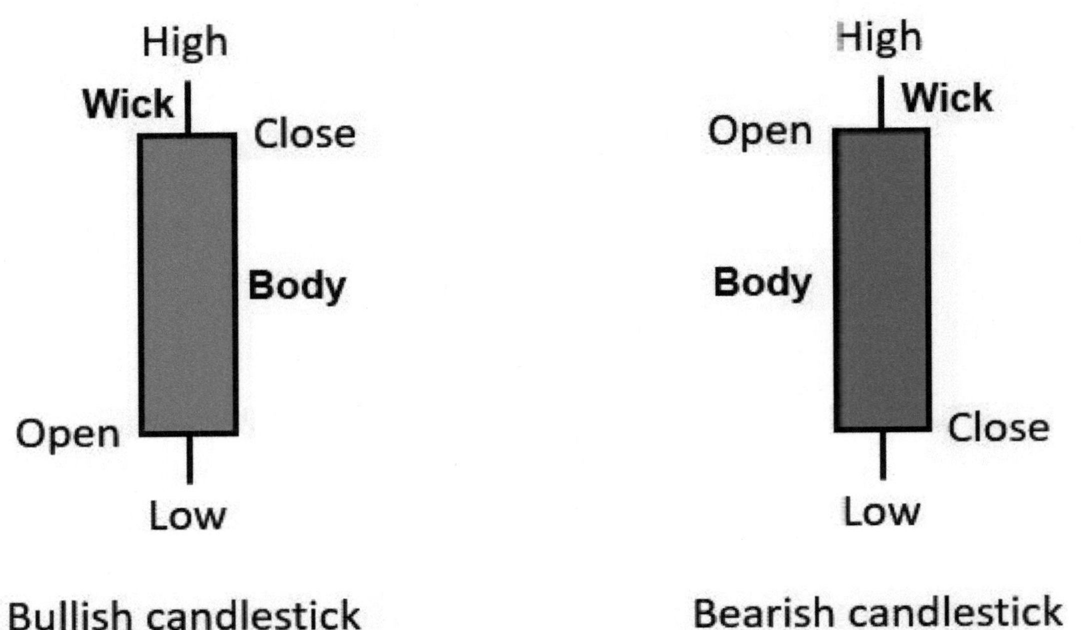

In this picture, you can see bullish and bearish candles. The green candle is a bullish candle and the red candle is a bearish candle. High and lows are the same in both candles. The bullish candle opens from the downside and closes to the upside. A bearish candle opens from the upside and closes to the downside.

These green and red parts are called the body. There's a wick on the upside and downside which shows the market went at that level. The other name of the wick is shadow. You can say any of them.

So, Why do we call them bullish and bearish candles and how did these candles get these names?

So, Bullish means bull and how the bull attacks, Downside to the upside

In this picture of the bull you can see how the bull attacks, He attacks downside to upside. Down to up means positive and this is why a green candle is called a bullish candle.

Now, Why did a bearish candle get its name?

Bearish means bear and how bear attacks, Upside to the downside.

Bear attacks upside to the downside. Up to down means negative and this is why red candle is called a bearish candle.

14:) Indicators and price action

Indicators means do indicate. It predicts what will be the next move of the market. For example:- You're going somewhere with a bike and now you are going to move left side and you give the indicator then other riders and drivers will understand what will be your next move.

Now, price action means trading without indicators like you have a naked chart like this

This is called a naked chart that you can see in this picture.

There are two types of price action:- Pure price action and not-so-pure price action.

Pure price action:- In pure price action we can't use indicators, We analyse the market on the naked chart.

Not-so-pure price action:- In not-so-pure price action, We analyse the market with help of indicators. We can use indicators just to confirm our analysis.

15:) RSI

RSI is an indicator and it helps us to find the trade. It stands for Relative Strength Index. Now, let's see how it can help us?

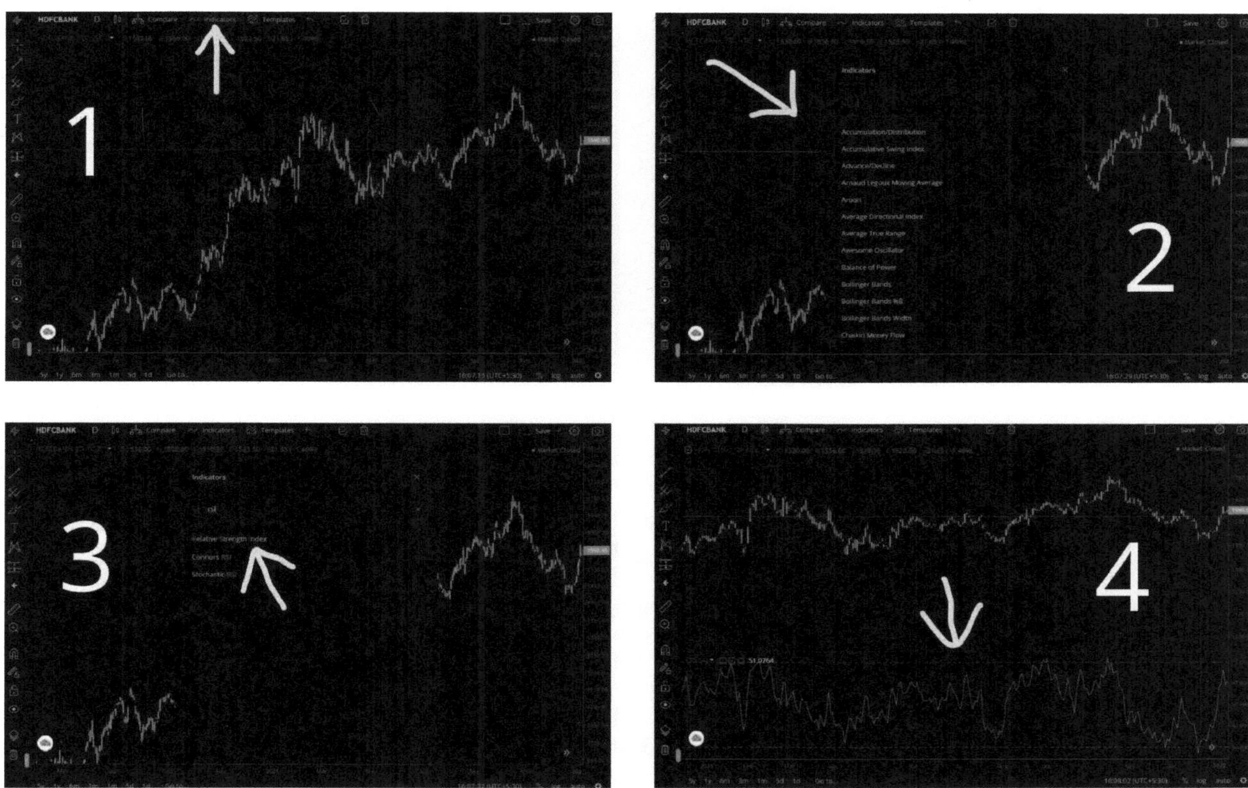

See in this picture, First of all click on indicators on the upside then a lot of indicators will open you can see there then search there RSI and click on it. After clicking there will be a box open in the downside.

Now, Let's see how this works?

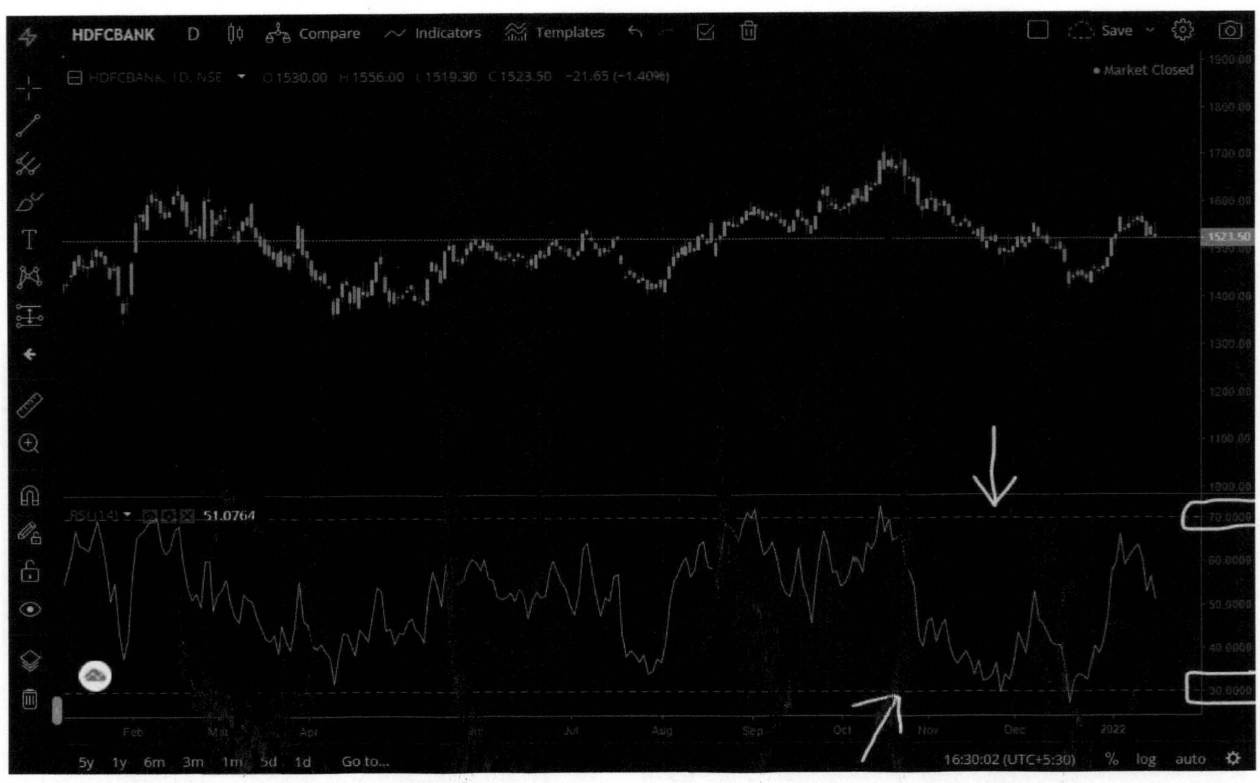

In this picture, you can see there are two horizontal lines. The first one is on the upside and the second one is on the downside. And you can see on the right side there are numbers. The first horizontal line is equal to 70 and the second horizontal line is equal to 30. If this line crosses the horizontal line of 70 then it means it is an overbought situation in the market and if this line crosses the horizontal line of 30 then it means it is an oversold situation in the market.

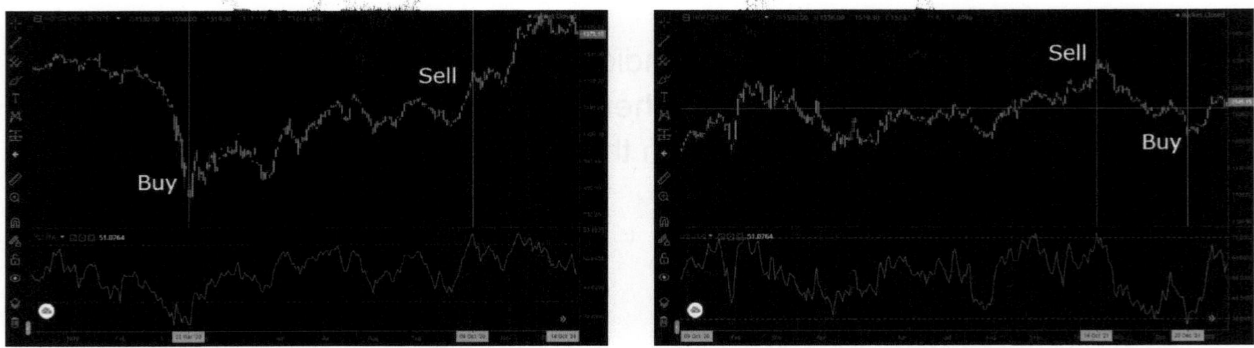

You can see in the picture how the market reacts to this RSI line and how you can trade with the help of RSI.

16:) Moving average

Moving average is also a great indicator and it's a lagging indicator. A lagging indicator means the market will move a little bit then it tells us what will be the next move of the market.

Let's see how it will help us to analyse the market.

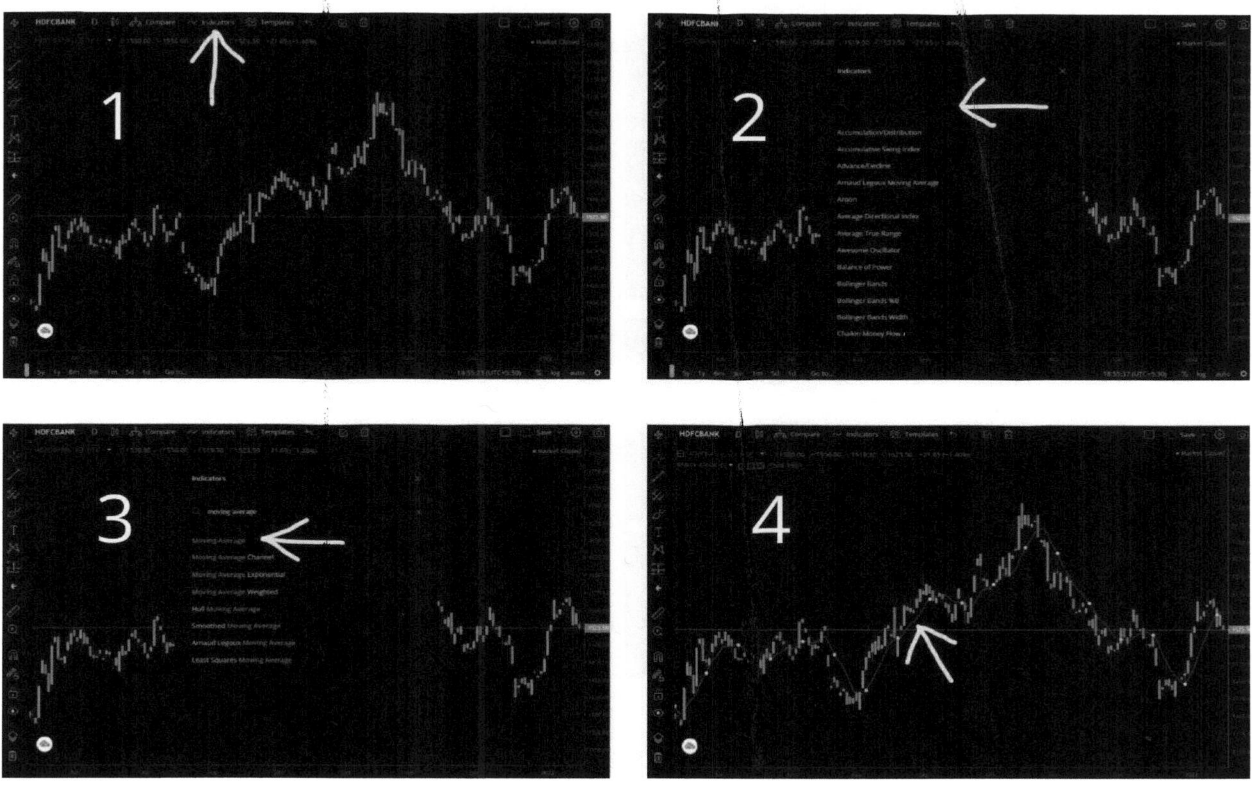

First of all you have to click on indicators on the upside then search in that box 'moving average' and then this line will come. This line is a moving average line.

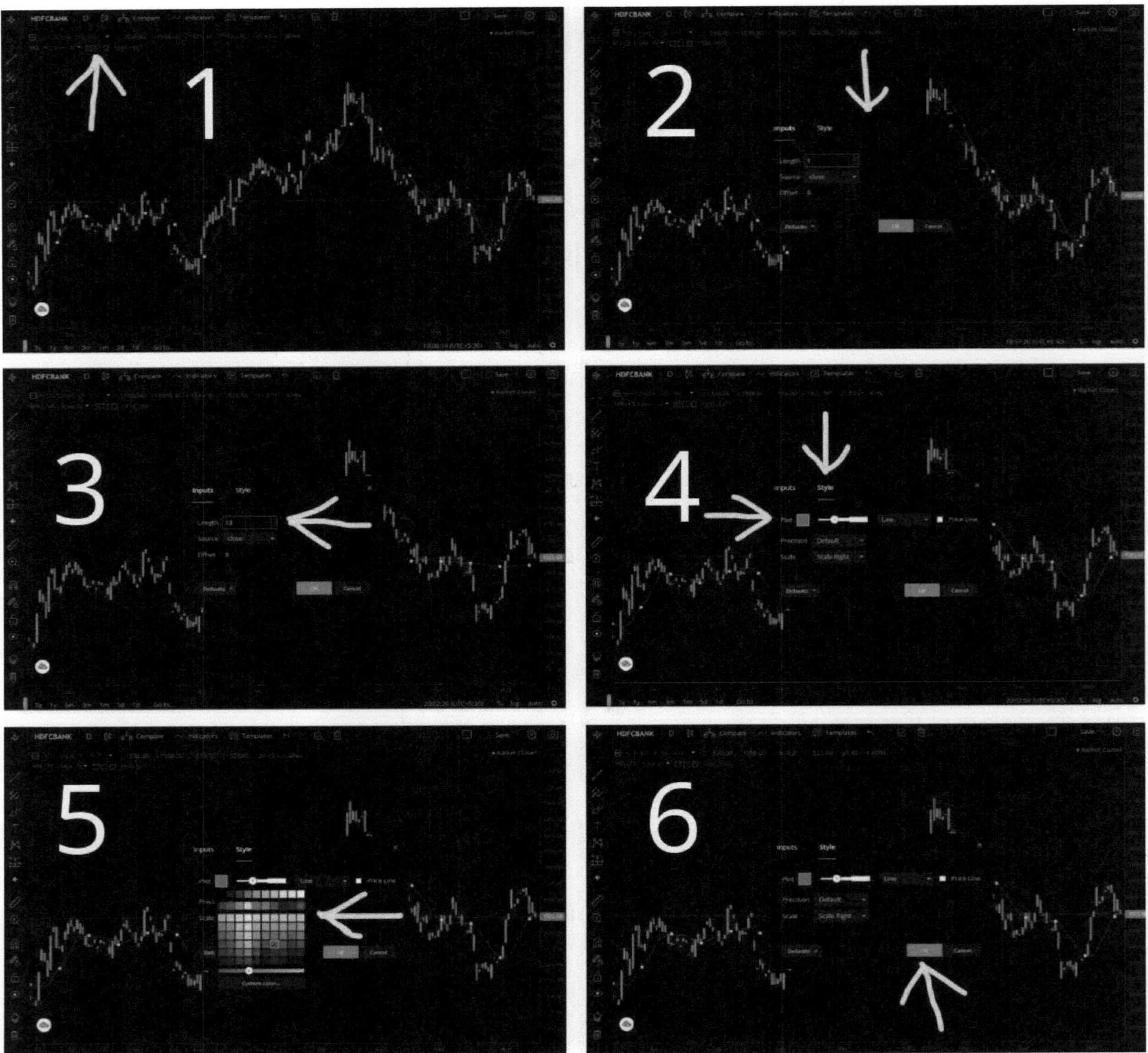

Then click on the gear icon then there is a length. Length and period are the same thing. If we put any number in length like we put 13 then that means the average of the last thirteen candles. After putting 13 there then click on the style and then color box then so many colors will open you can choose whichever you like and then click OK.

If that moving average line is below the price then that means it is an uptrend and if that line is above the price then that means it is a downtrend.

Now, add another moving average to analyse the market in an easy way.

The process is the same, Click on indicators then click on moving average and then click on the gear icon then type 17 in length and then choose the color and then click on OK.

If both lines cross each other and then turn their face on the upside then there should be a buy position and if both cross each other again then you should sell.

Similarly, If both lines cross each other and then turn their face on the downside then there should be a sell position and if both cross each other again then you should buy.

17:) Volume

The volume shows the liquidity in the market. Liquidity means how many people are trading in the market and how many people did trade on one candle.

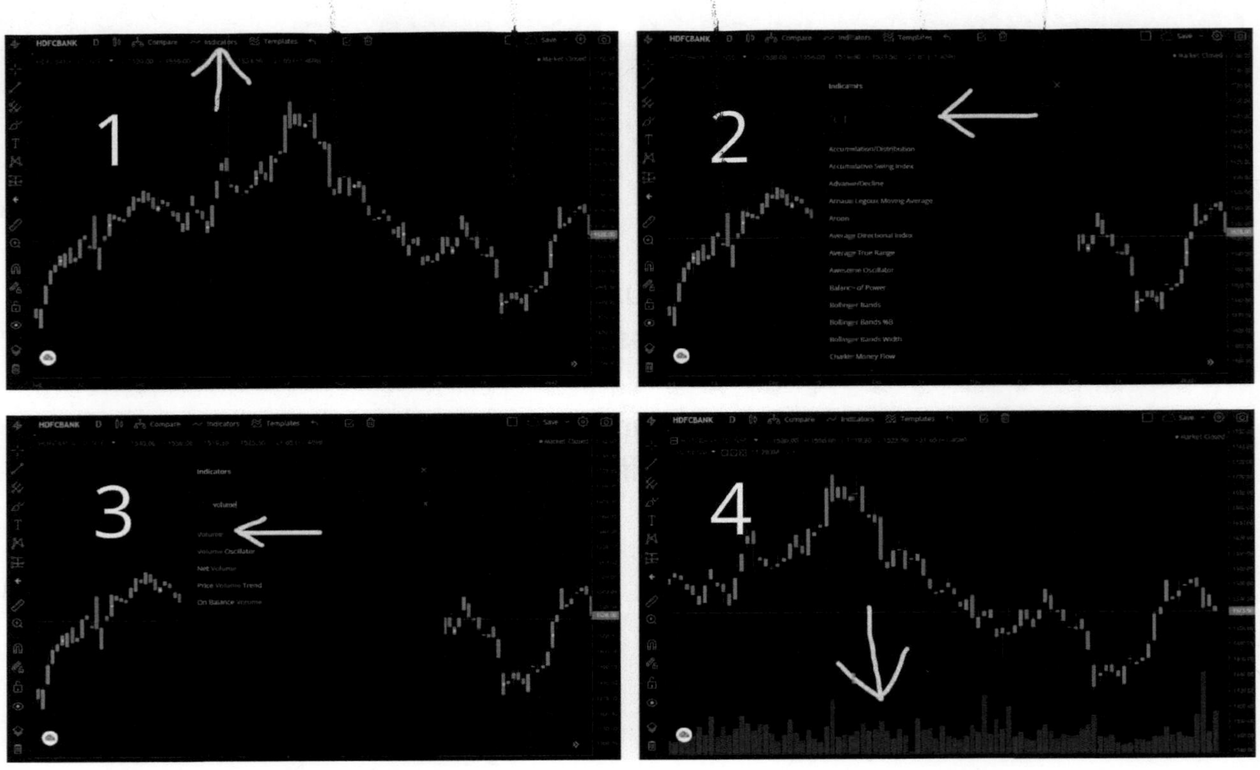

Click on the indicator then search 'volume' there then click on volume and then you can see on the downside that is volume.

If you put your crosshair on any candle then you can see on the upside volume that shows how many people did trade on a single candle.

18:) Trendline

Trendline is a thing which works like support and resistance. It is part of the price action. From here our price action journey has started. In price action, we analyse the market without indicators.

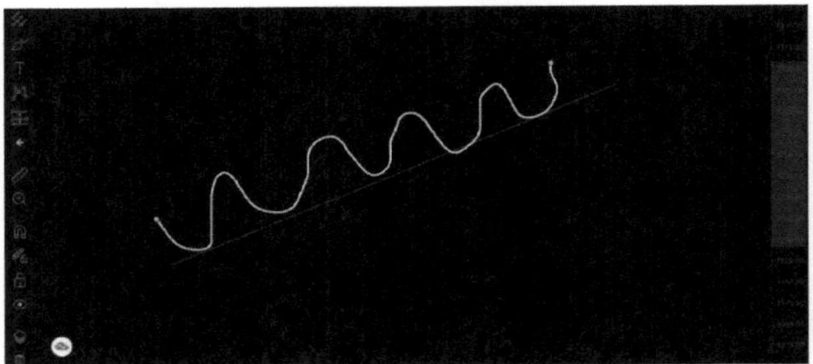

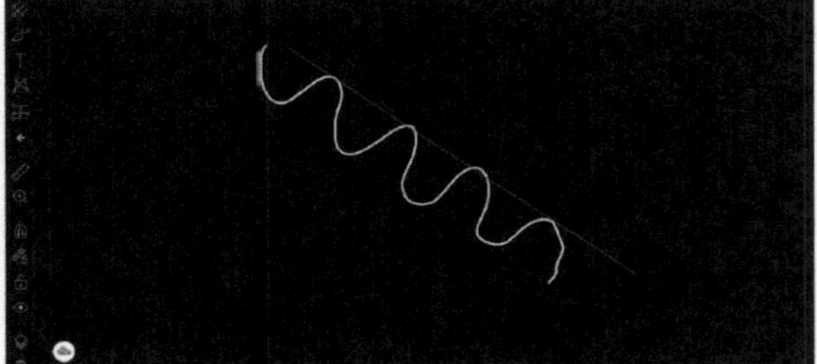

In this picture, I drew an uptrend and downtrend and then drew a trendline from the left side. So, this is a line where the market gives us entries and exits. This line is called trendline.

Trendline means a line which follows the trend.

Now, I am gonna show you an example.

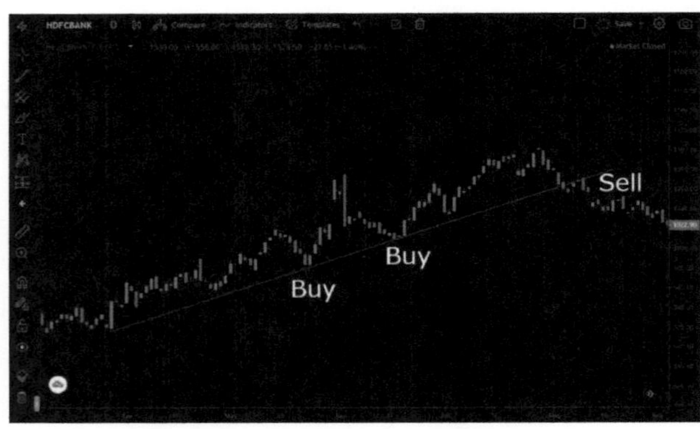

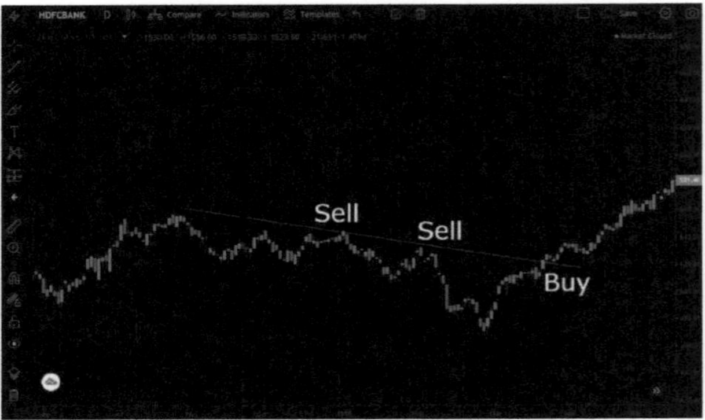

Look how this trendline respects the market. The market is in an uptrend and it breaks the trendline to the downside then there should be a sell position. Similarly, The market is in a downtrend and it breaks the trendline to the upside then there should be a buy position. Zoom out the chart to find trendlines easily.

19:) Support and resistance

Support and resistance are another part of price action. It is a powerful tool of price action. I will make you understand support and resistance.

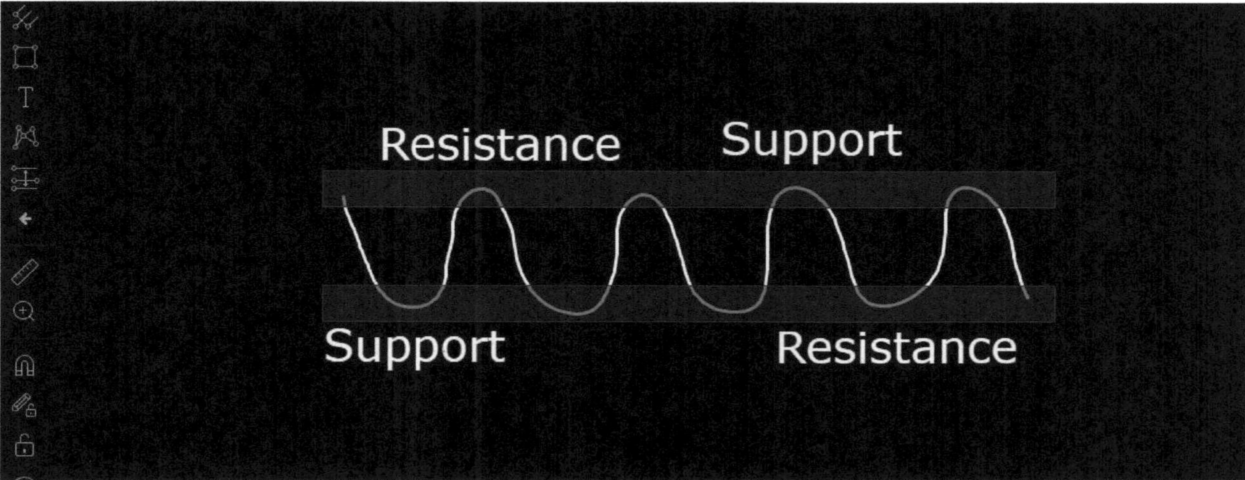

In this picture, you can see that I drew a line and then drew zones. These zones are support and resistance zones. If the market goes downside to the upside then the part of the downside works as support and part of the upside works as resistance.
And if the market goes upside to the downside then the part of the upside as support and part of the downside works as resistance.

Now, I am gonna show you an example.

Look in this picture how the market respects these zones.

First, there is a support in this picture on the downside and there is a resistance on the upside and the market was roaming between these zones then the market broke that zone and resistance became support.

Remember one thing that the support and resistance will always be zones these won't be line like trendlines. And these zones will always be horizontal.

Zoom out the chart to find support and resistance easily.

20:) Dynamic support and resistance

Dynamic support and resistance is an interesting tool to find support and resistance. It is an easy way to do technical analysis. This support and resistance tool is an indicator and this is an exponential moving average. The short form is EMA.

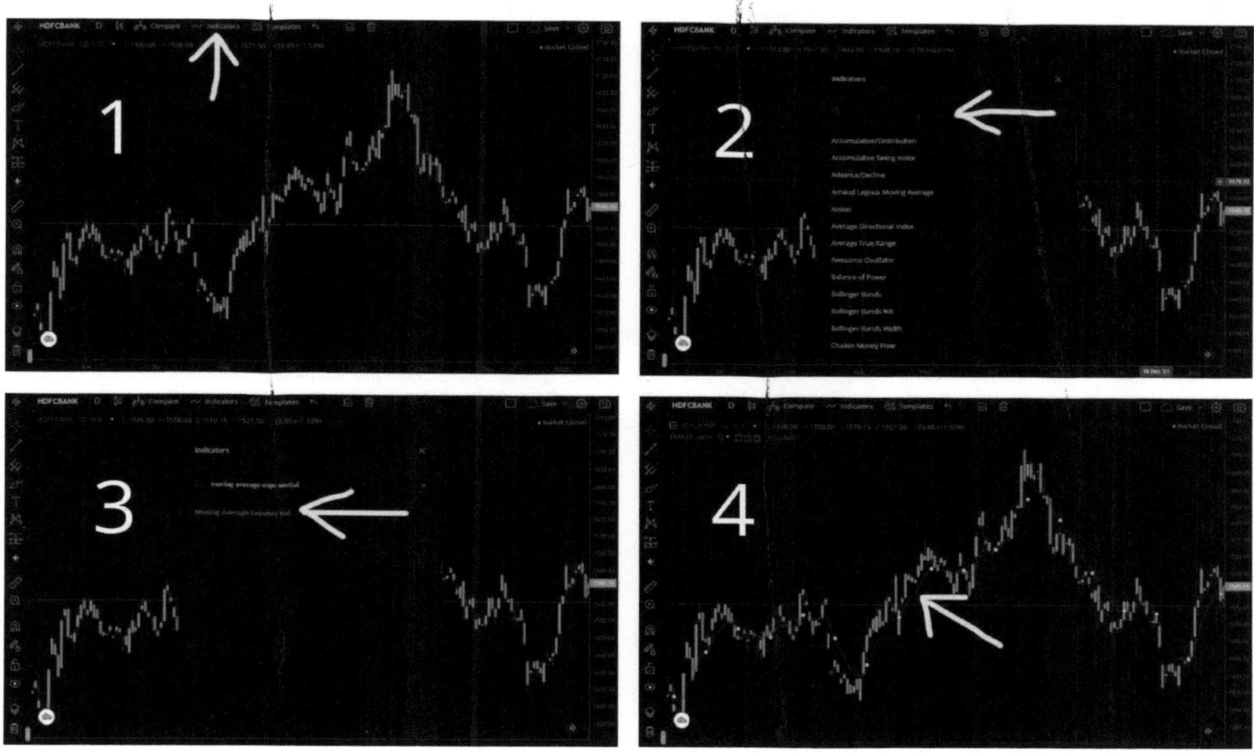

Click on indicators then search there 'exponential moving average' then click on it and then an EMA line will come.

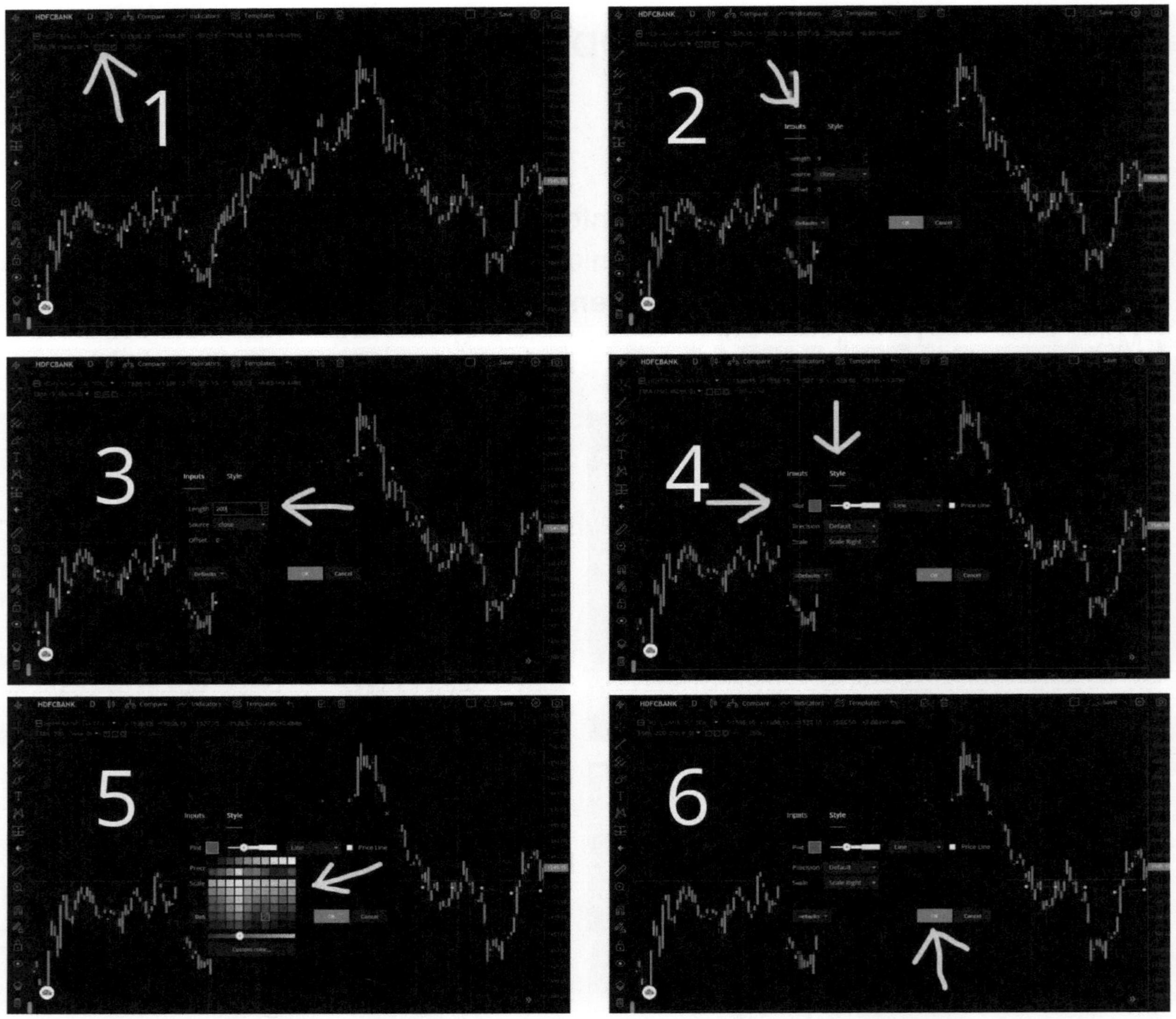

Then click on the gear icon then type there 200 then click on style then click on color icon then choose the color and then click OK.

If the market is above the EMA line then that means it's an uptrend and if the market is below the EMA line then that means it's a downtrend. This EMA line works like support and resistance.

I drew a drawing and then drew a 200 EMA line. Look how it works like support and resistance.

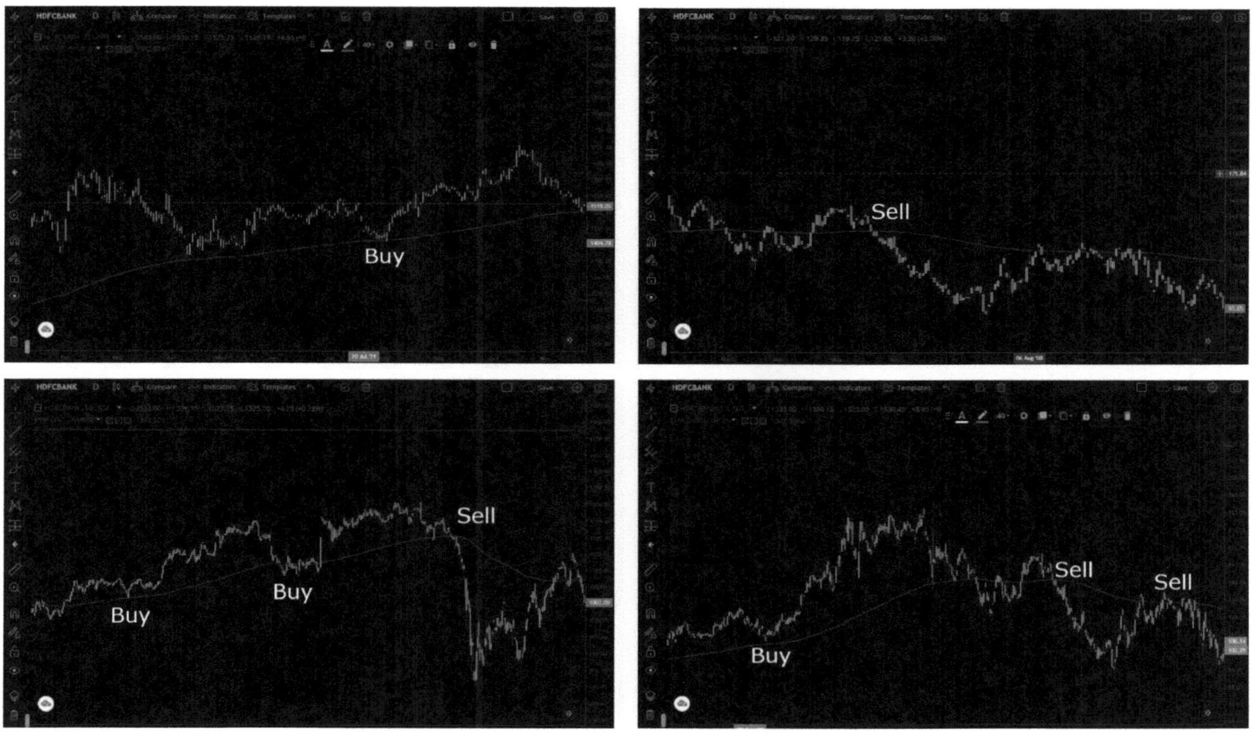

In this picture, you can see how it works. How you can find support and resistance.

21:) Fibonacci retracement

Fibonacci retracement is a mathematical tool invented by Leonardo Fibonacci in the 13th century. It also works as support and resistance. There are some ratios where the market takes support and resistance. 23%, 38%, 50%, 61% and 78% these are ratios.

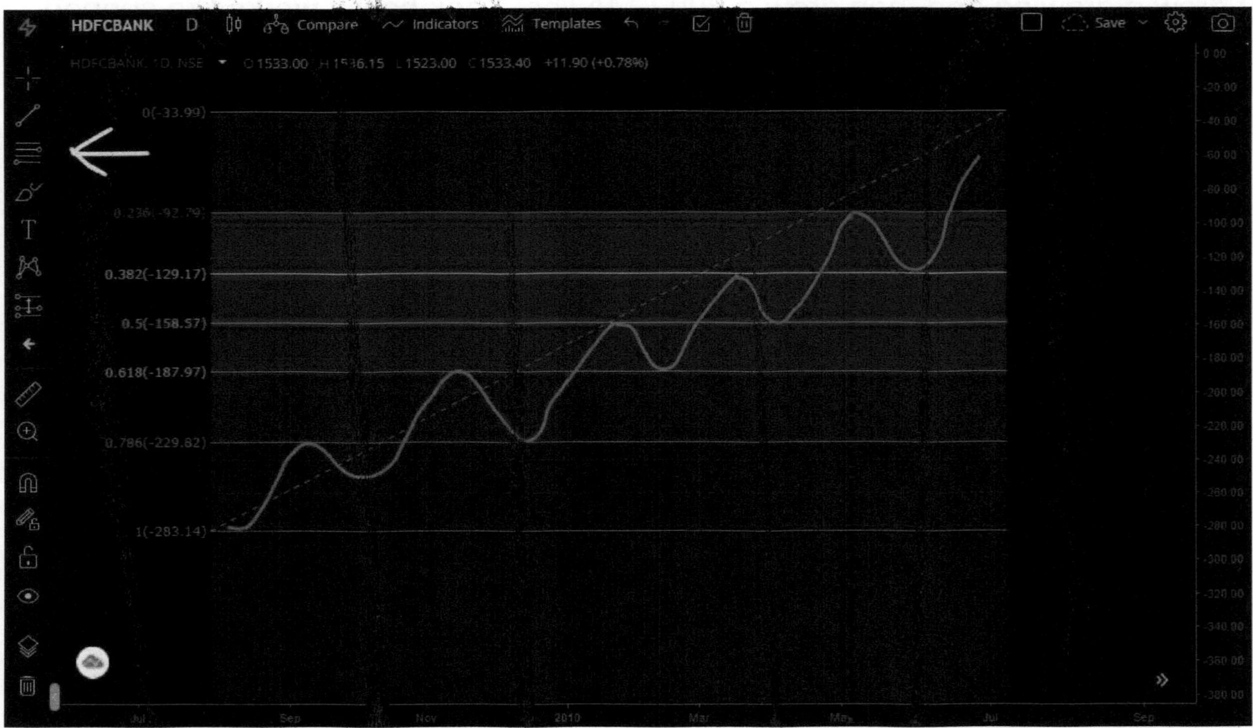

I drew market structure and then drew fibonacci retracement. Click on the left fibonacci icon for drawing fibonacci retracement. You can see in this picture how the market respects fibonacci retracement. You have to connect low to high and high to low for drawing fibonacci retracement.

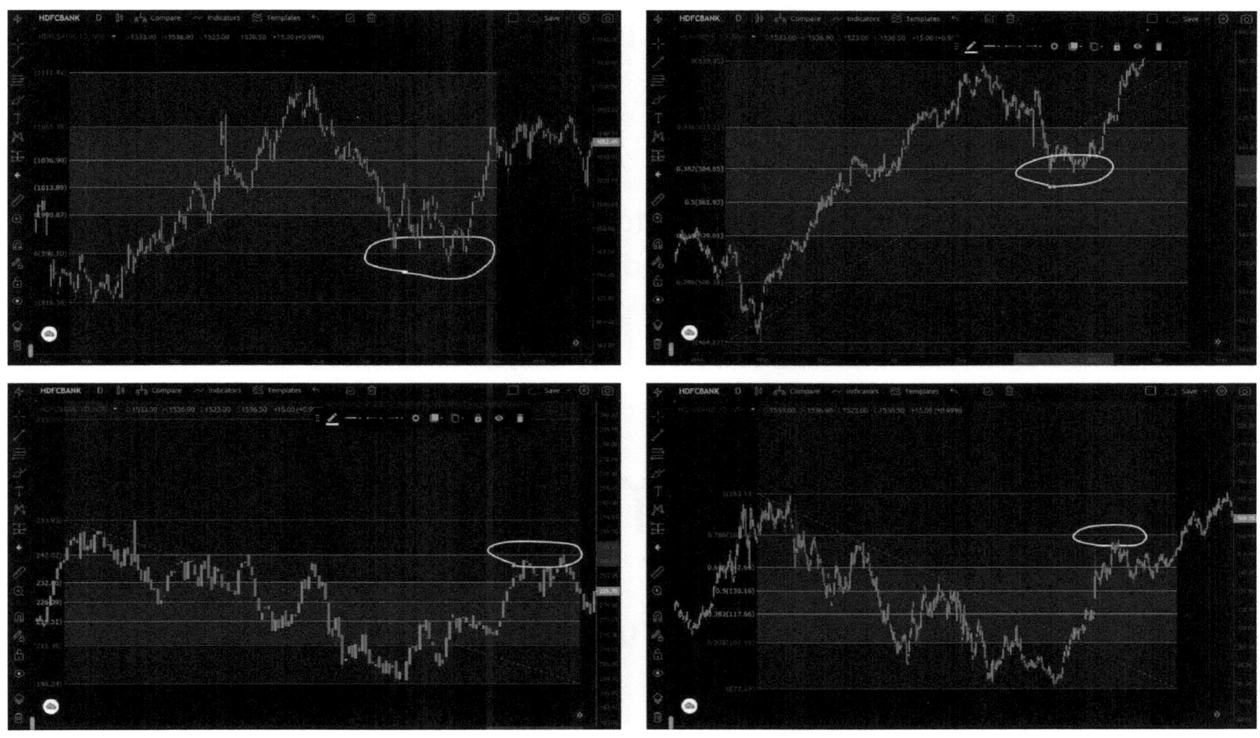

In these pictures, you can see how fibonacci retracement works. It is not necessary that the market takes rejection at every level. And 61% is the golden ratio because the market often takes rejection at that level.

For example:-

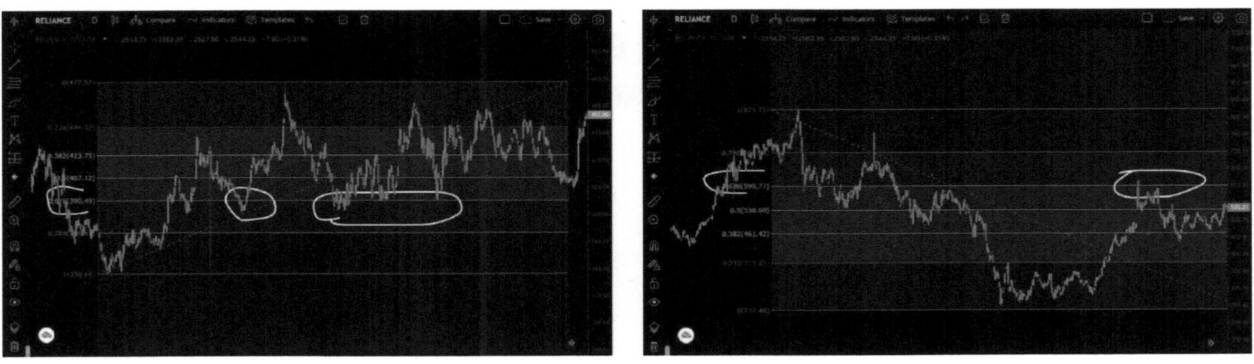

Look how the market is taking rejection at the level of 61%. This is how fibonacci retracement helps us.

22:) Candlesticks

Candlesticks are another powerful way to do technical analysis. I will tell you about candles and make you understand how it works.

Hammer:- First candlestick in our list is a hammer. Let's see how it looks like.

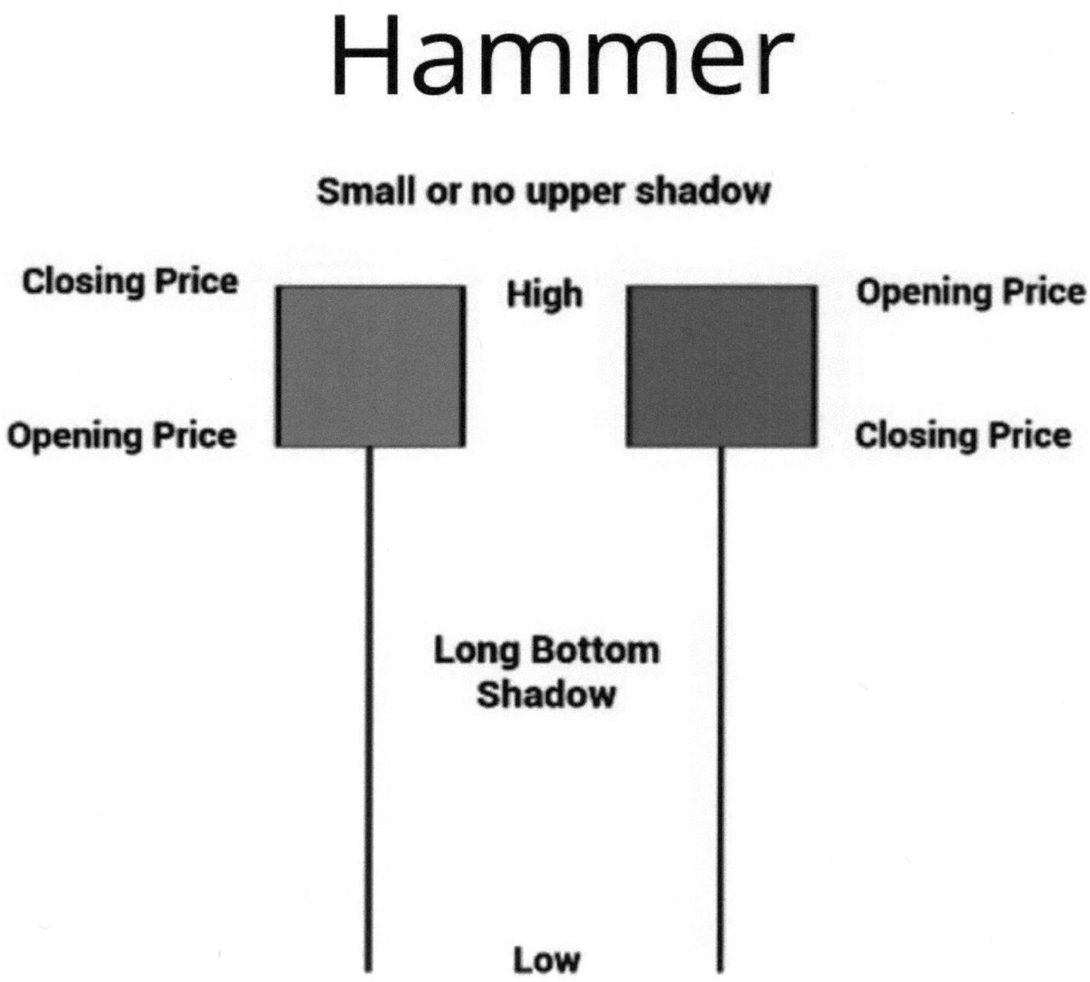

Hammer

Small or no upper shadow

Closing Price

High

Opening Price

Opening Price

Closing Price

Long Bottom Shadow

Low

In this picture, you can see this hammer. The identification of the hammer is that the shadow should be long and the body should be small. Hammer should come from the downside. Hammer can be red or green both are genuine.

Now, Let’s see the hammer in the chart.

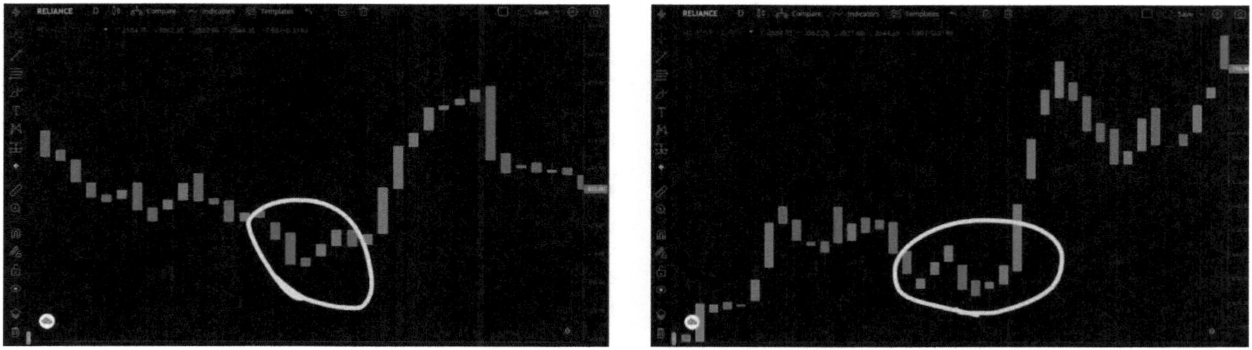

In this picture, you can see the hammer came then the market went up.

Shooting star:- Our second candlestick is shooting star.

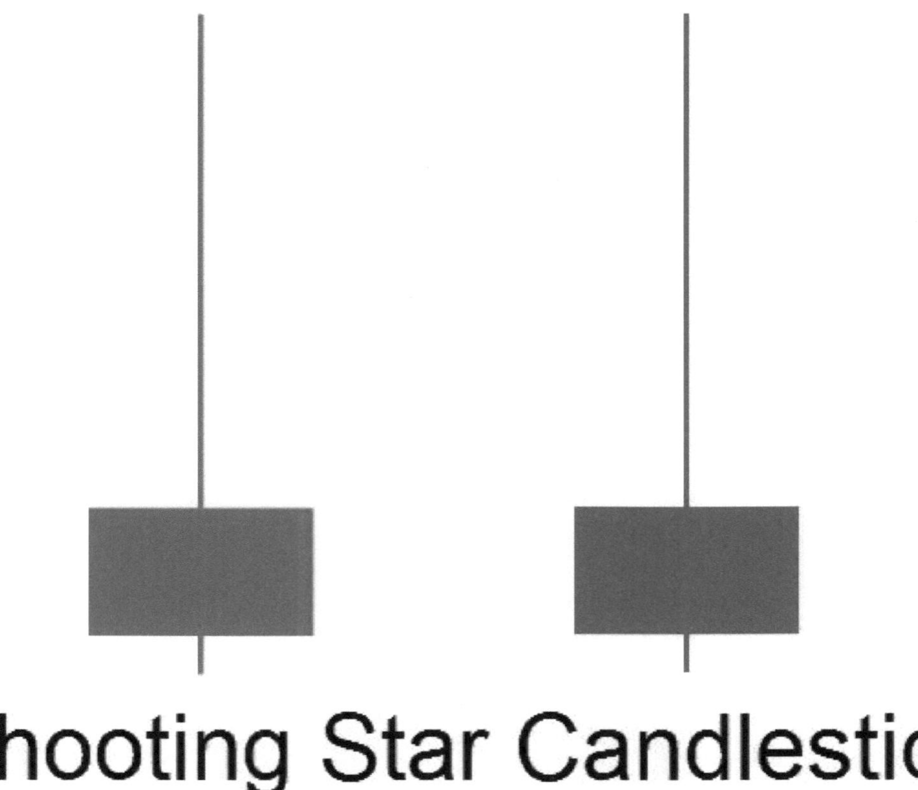

This is a shooting star candlestick and it comes on the upside. Shooting star pushes down the market. It can be red or green.

Let's see in the chart:-

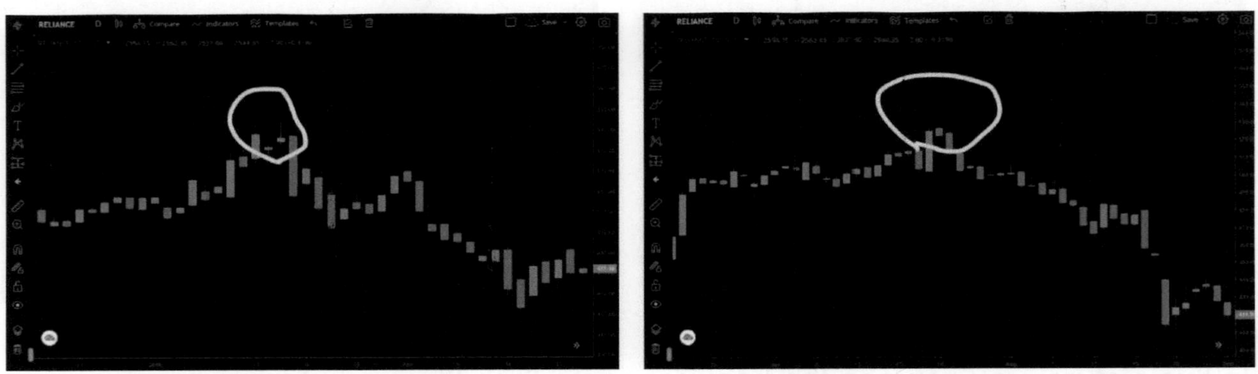

Look shooting star came and then the market went down.

Spinning top:- Our next candlestick is spinning top.

In the spinning top, The body should be between the shadow and it should be small. If it comes on the upside then it means the market will go down and if it comes on downside then it means the market will go up.

Let's see the spinning top in the chart:-

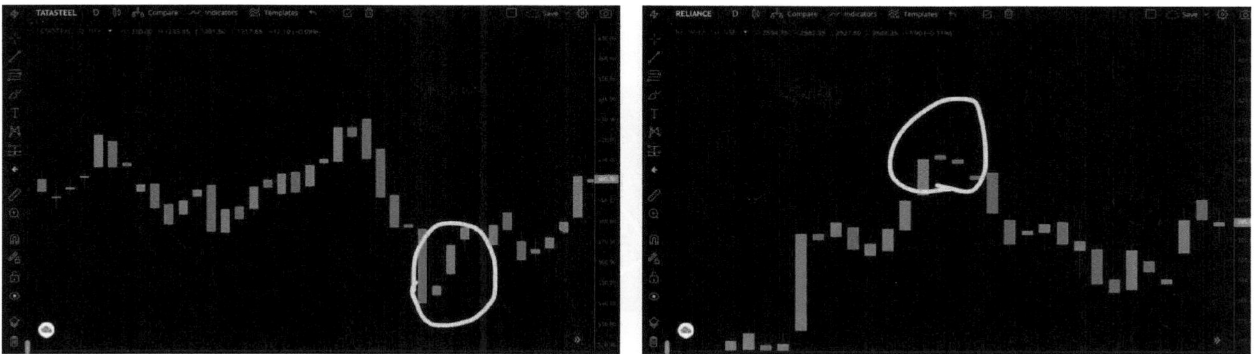

Look how it works.

Doji:- Next candlestick is doji.

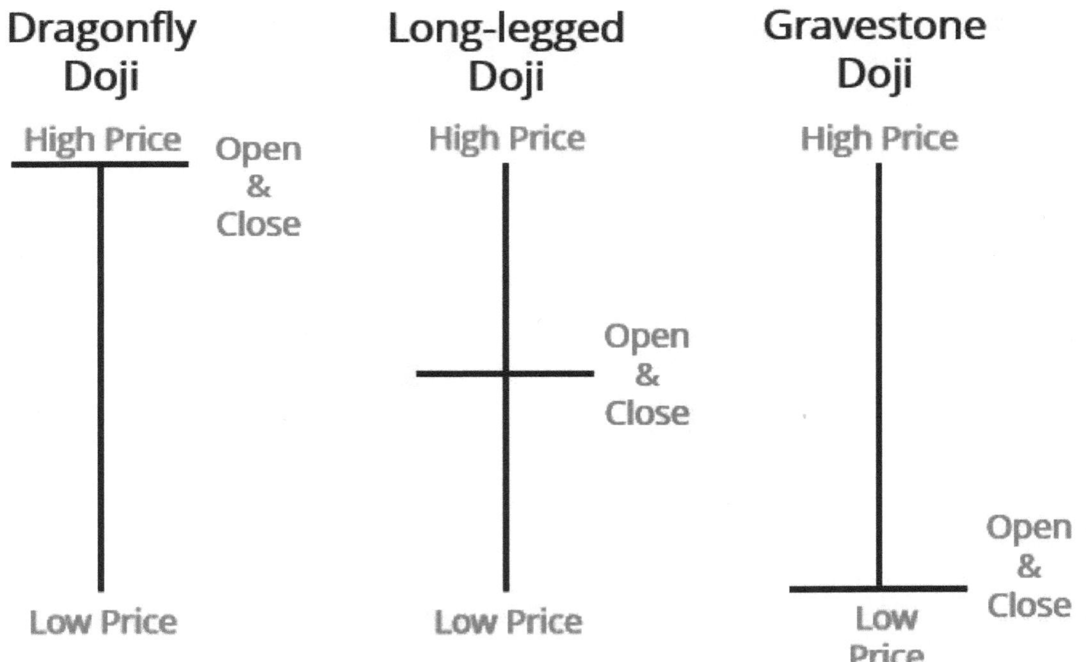

There are three types of doji:- Dragonfly doji, Long-legged doji and gravestone doji. Open and close should be on the same level. The shadow should be long.

The body should be on the upside in dragonfly doji, The body should be between the shadow in long-legged doji and the body should be on the downside in the gravestone doji.

Let's see in the chart:-

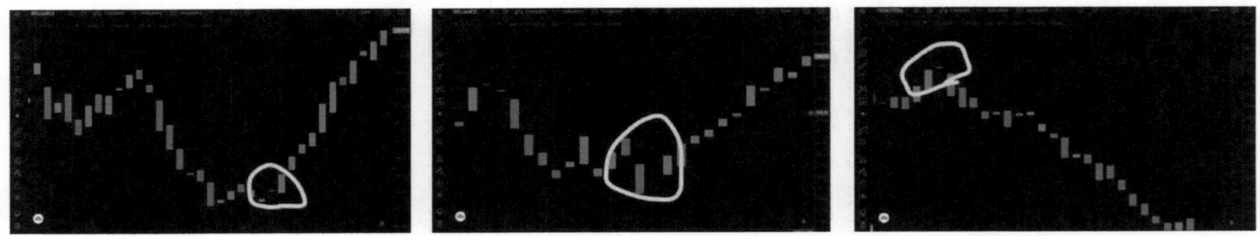

Dragonfly doji looks like a hammer, long-legged doji locks like a spinning top and gravestone doji looks like a shooting star. But the body will be too small in doji.

Bullish engulfing:- Our next candlestick is bullish engulfing.

Bullish engulfing

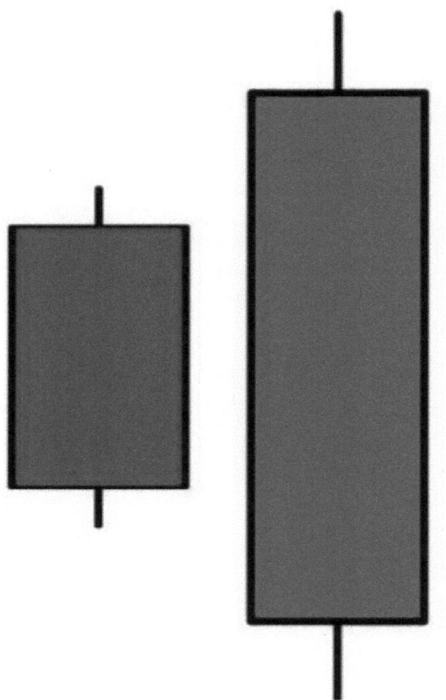

Bullish engulfing is the combination of two candles. The first candle should be red, the second candle should be green. The green candle should be longer than the red candle.

The interpretation is simple that if this comes from the downside then the market will go up.

Let's see in the chart:-

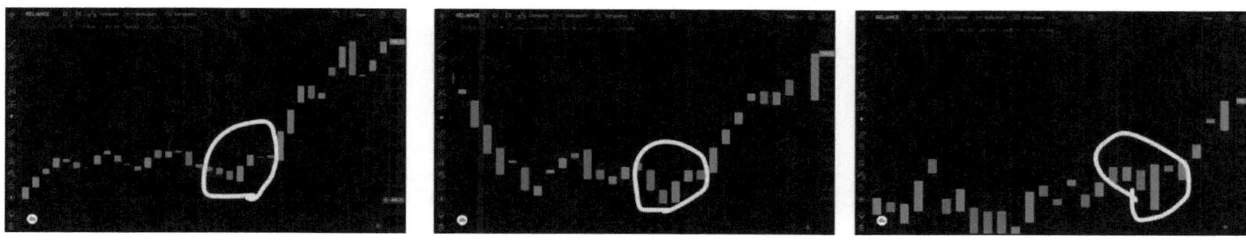

Bearish engulfing:- Our next candlestick is bearish engulfing.

Bearish engulfing

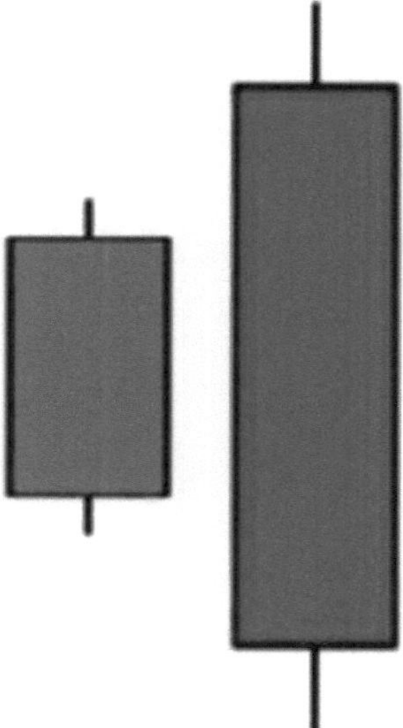

The first candle should be green in bearish engulfing and the second candle should be red. The red candle should be longer than the green candle. If it comes from the upside then the market will go down.

Let's see in the chart:-

Bullish harami:- Our next candlestick is bullish harami.

Bullish harami

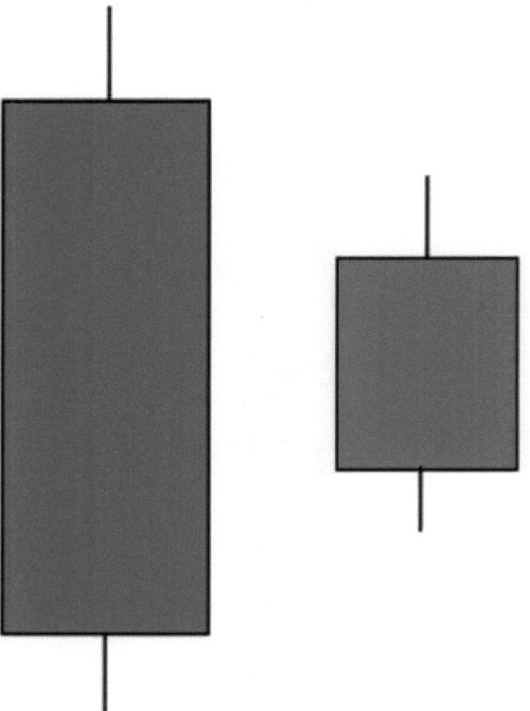

Bullish harami is the combination of two candles. The first candle should be red and the second candle should be green. The green candle should be smaller than the red candle. If it comes from the downside then the market will go up.

Let's see in the chart:-

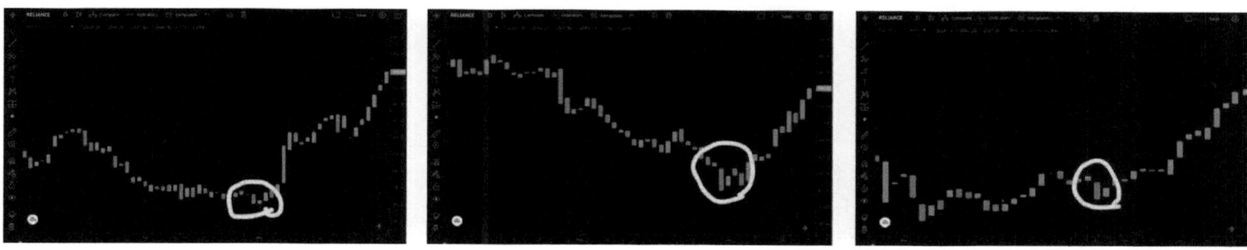

Bearish harami:- Our final candlestick is bearish harami.

Bearish harami

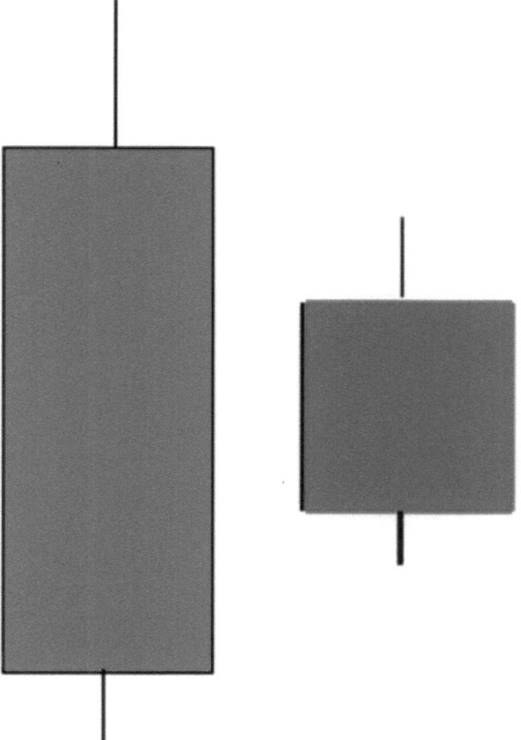

In bearish harami, the first candle should be green and the second candle should be red. The red candle should be smaller than the green candle. If it comes from the upside then the market will go down.

Let's see in the chart:-

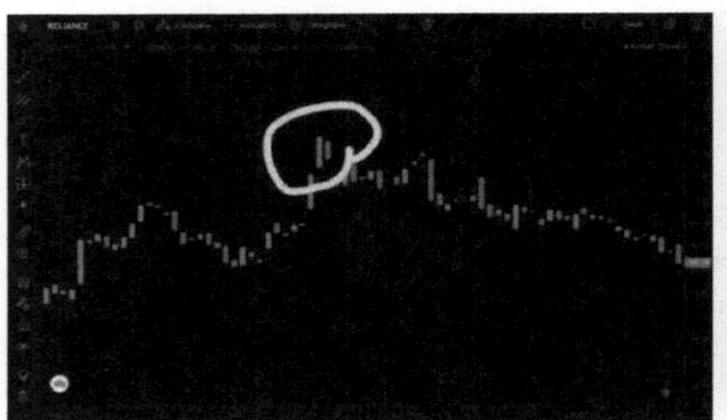 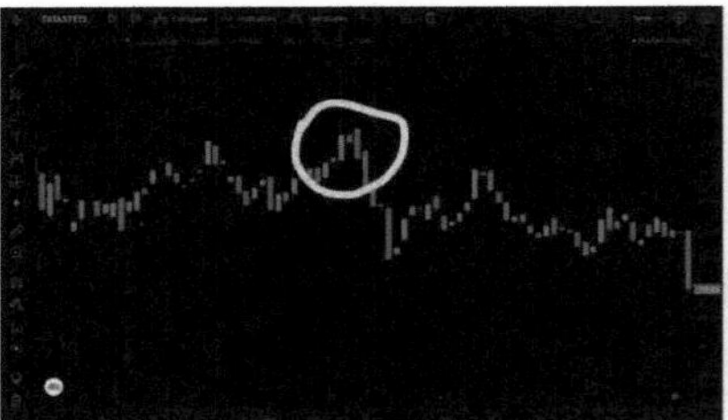 

23:) Chart patterns

Chart patterns are the important thing for price action. I will tell you about chart patterns.

Double top:- So, Our first chart pattern is double top. Let's see how it looks like.

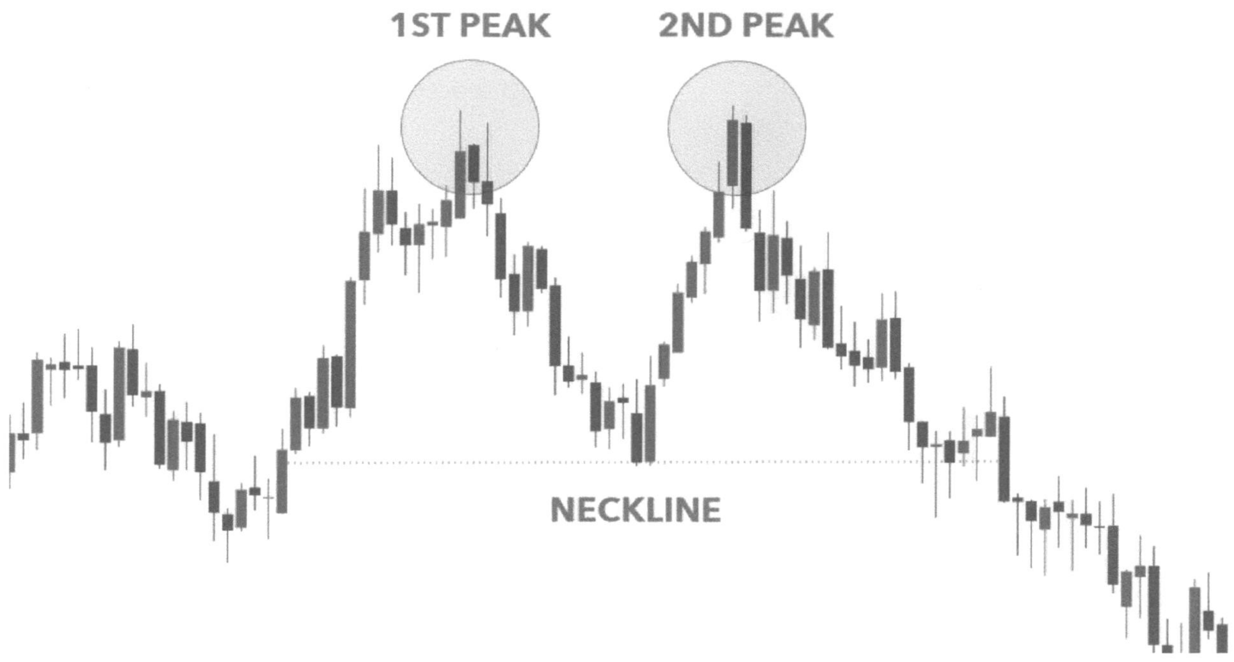

Look there's a first top and then second top and after that the market went down. If this pattern comes then that means the market will go down.

Now, let's see in the chart:-

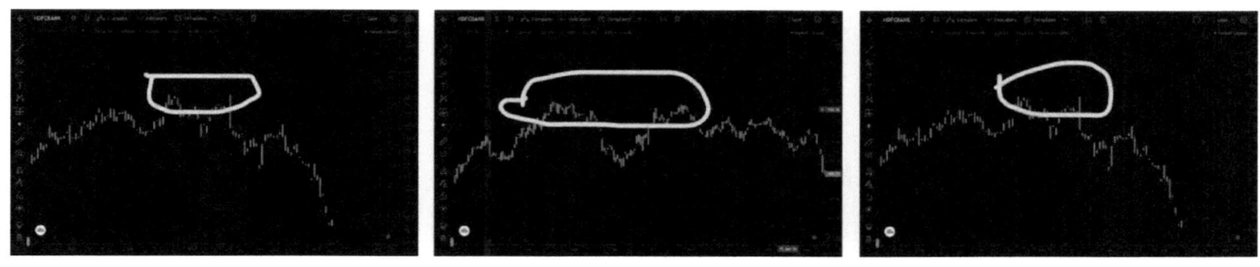

Look in the picture how the double top works.

Double bottom:- Our second chart pattern is the double bottom. If this pattern comes from the downside then that means the market will go up. Let's see how it looks like.

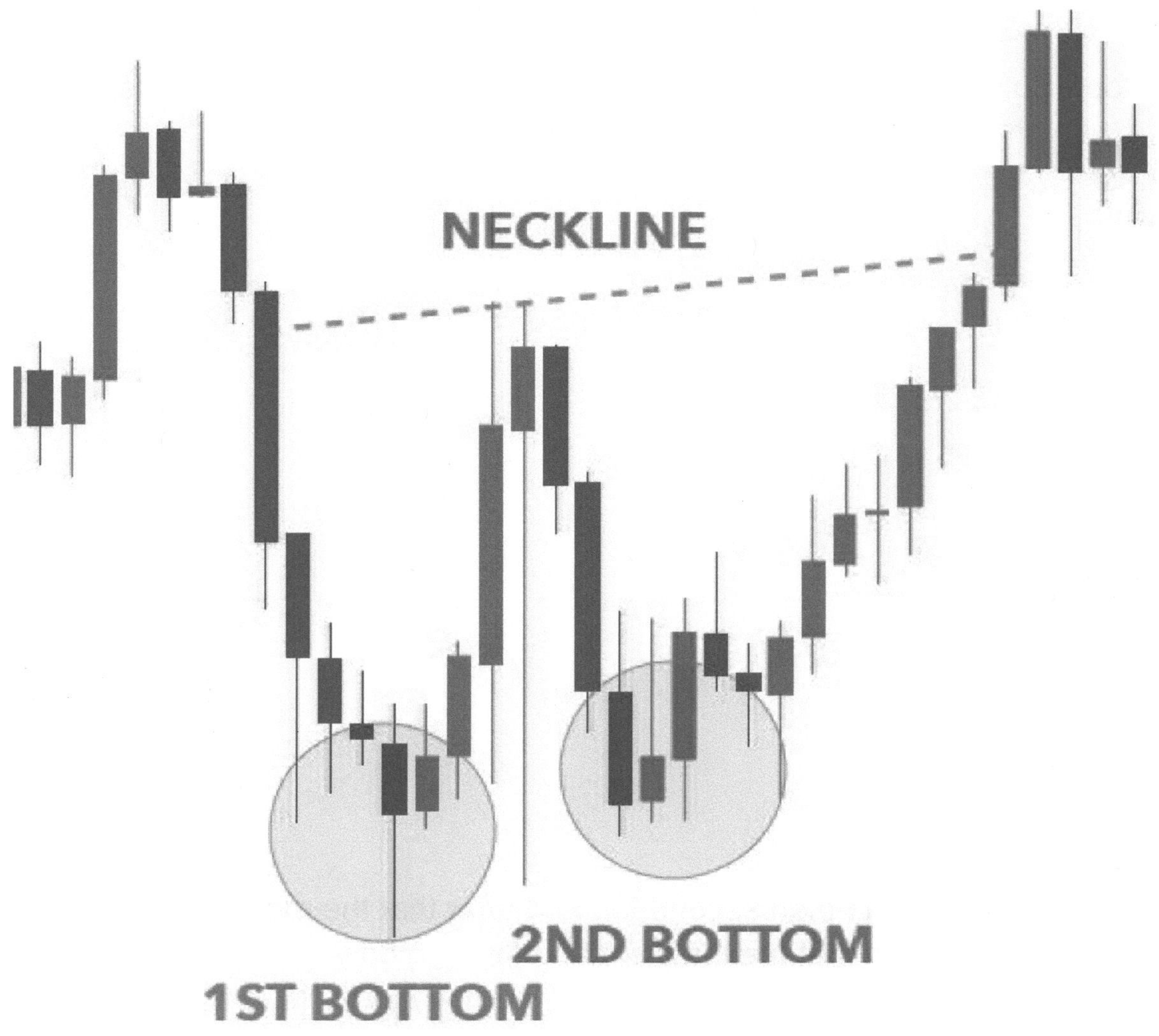

Now, Let's see in the chart:-

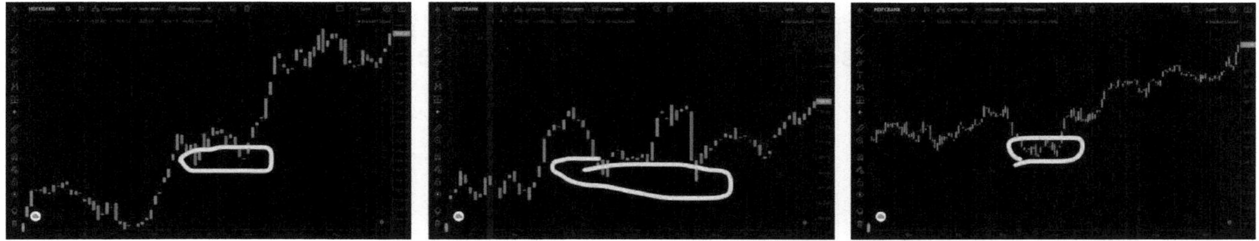

Falling wedge:- Our next pattern is falling wedge. Let's see how it looks like.

A falling wedge is the combination of two trendlines. First, you have to draw a trendline which connects to highs then draw the second line which connects to lows. If the market breaks a trendline on the upside then that means the market will go up.

Now, Let's see in the chart:-

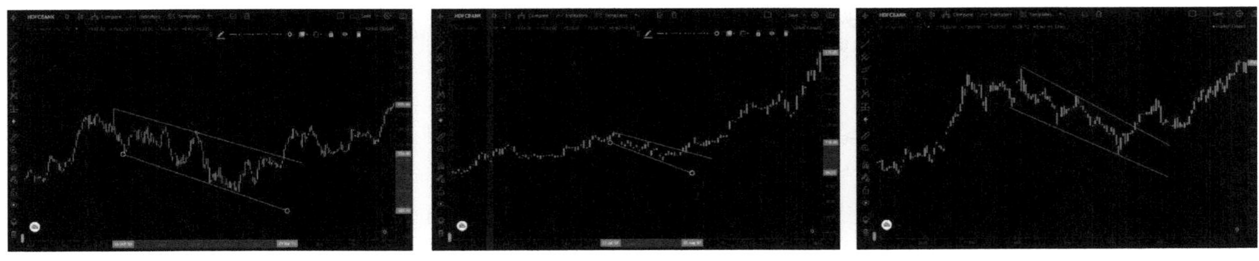

Rising wedge:- Our next pattern is the rising wedge. Let's see how it looks like.

A rising wedge is also the combination of two trendlines. First, you have to draw a trendline which connects to lows then draw the second line which connects to highs. If the market breaks a trendline to the downside then that means the market will go down.

Let's see in the chart:-

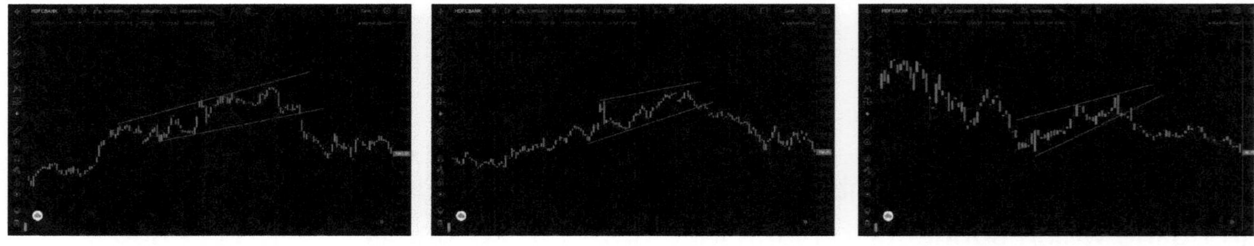

Head & shoulders:- This is the most powerful chart pattern. In this pattern, there are two shoulders and a head. This chart pattern comes from the upside. If it comes and the neckline breaks then the market will go down.

Now, let's see how it looks like:-

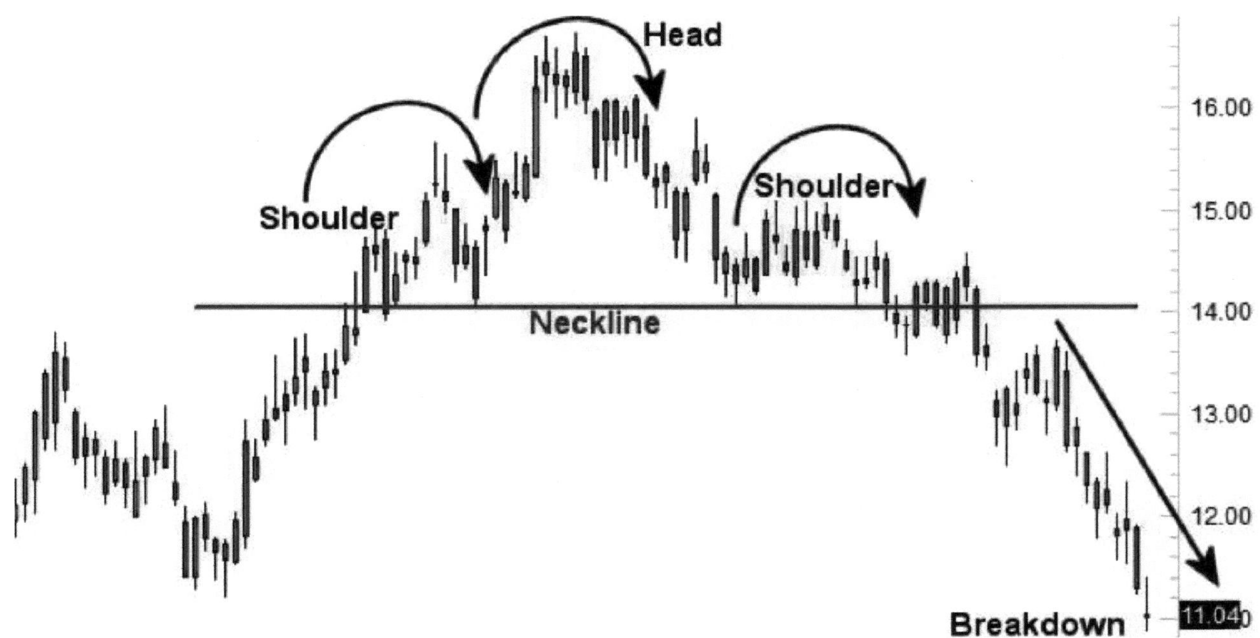

In this pattern, The first left shoulder will come then a head and then a right shoulder. There's a neckline and if the market breaks the neckline then the market will go down.

Now, let's see in the chart:-

Inverse head & shoulders:- This pattern is opposite to head & shoulders. This chart pattern comes from the downside. If it comes and the neckline breaks then the market will go up.

Now, let's see how it looks like:-

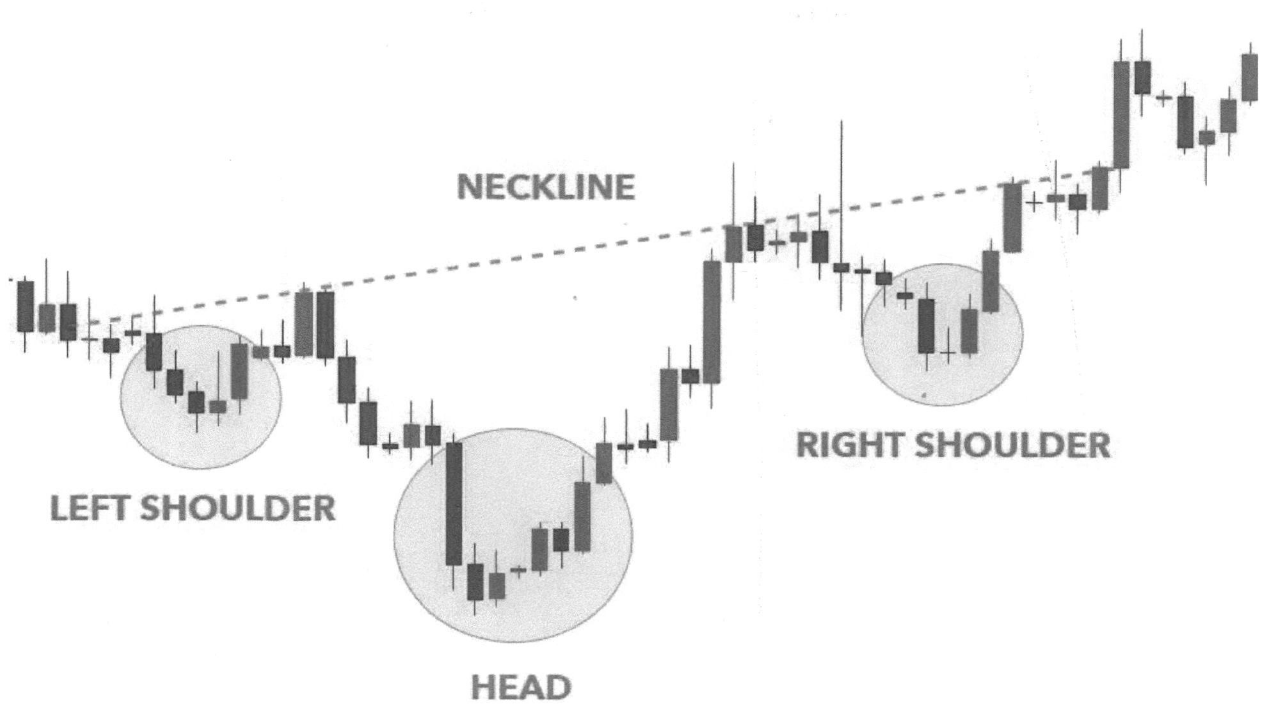

This is an inverted head & shoulders. There's a left shoulder then a head and then a right shoulder.

Now, let's see in the chart:-

Symmetrical:- This chart pattern looks like a triangle.

Let's see how it looks like:-

As I said, It looks like a triangle. Price becomes smaller in this pattern then the market either breaks up or breaks down in this pattern. If it breaks up then the market will go up and if it breaks down then the market will go down.

Now, Let's see in the chart:-

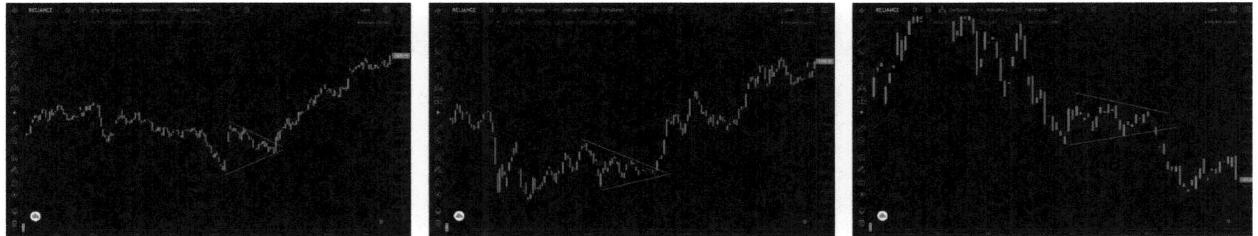

24:) How to avoid fake breakouts?

In this chapter, We will learn how to avoid fakeouts or fake breakouts?

I am going to teach you three methods. These three methods will help you to avoid fake breakouts.

The first method is that let the pattern fill and make itself. So, if any pattern is filling and it breaks before the end of that pattern then there are many chances that this is a fake breakout.

Let's understand it with an example.

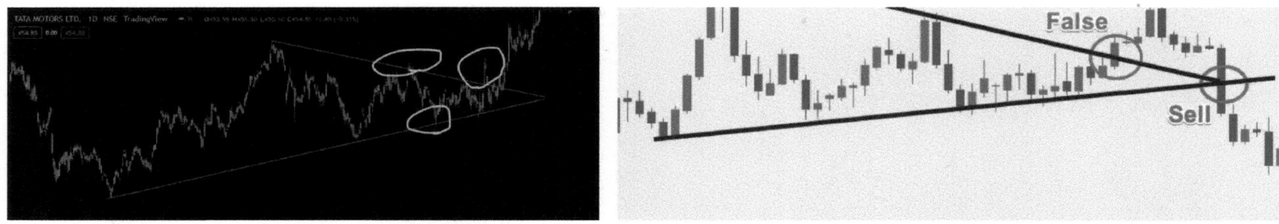

In this picture, you can see how fake breakouts look like and we can avoid these. So, The first method is that let the fill pattern itself properly.

Now, The second method for avoiding fake breakouts is let the candle complete itself. It does not matter which timeframe you use but al you have to do just let the candle complete itself.

Let's understand it with a picture.

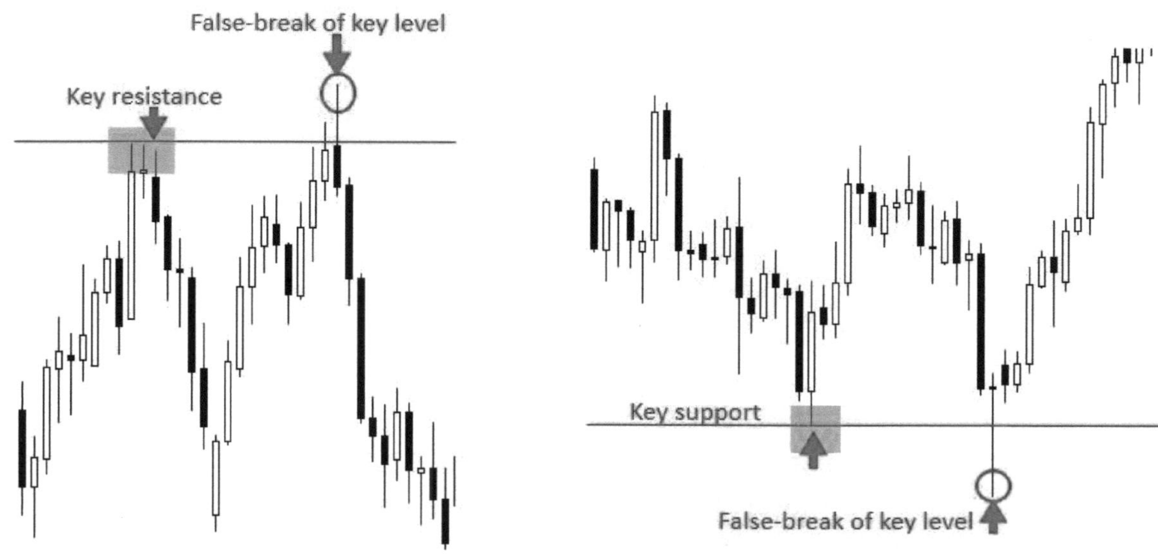

In this picture, we can clearly see that there is a double top pattern and before completing the candle if we took the buy trade then it would have definitely affected us.

Now, The third method for avoiding fake breakouts is the EMA of 200.

Yes, The EMA of 200 helps us to avoid fake breakouts. Let me show you how

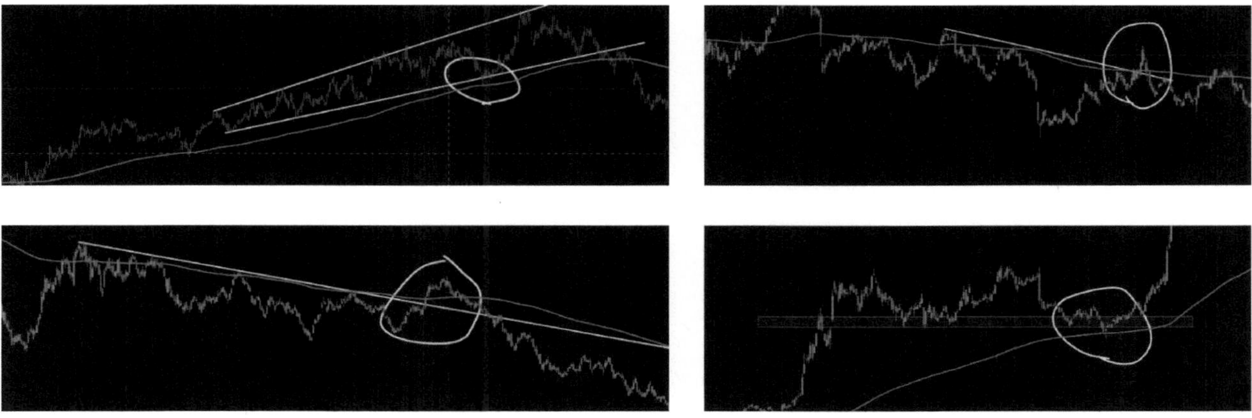

In these pictures, You can see that how EMA of 200 helps us to avoid fake breakouts. This is the best way to find fake breakouts.

Risk management and money management

25:) Risk-to-reward ratio

Risk-to-reward ratio means how much risk you have to take and how much reward you will get.

There are many types of ratios like 1:1, 1:2, 1:3 etc.

A 1:1 ratio means your risk and reward both are the same.

For example:- you took the trade into 'XYZ' whose share price is ₹300 and you put your stop loss at ₹250 and you take at ₹350. This is a 1:1 ratio.

Another example:- A share price of 'XYZ' is ₹300 and you took the buy trade in it. You put your stop loss at ₹250 and your take profit at ₹400. So, this is the risk-to-reward ratio. This is the 1:2 ratio. Your reward is higher than your risk.

The risk-to-reward ratio is an easy chapter. All you need to understand that how much is your risk and how much is your reward.

26:) Money management

The definition of this word is quite simple. Managing our money is money management.

If you are going to travel somewhere and you planned your budget, This is money management. Managing expenses, planning budget and etc.

For example:- Your salary is ₹1,00,000 and now let's manage this money. We put ₹40,000 for your monthly expenses like electricity and water bill, grocery items, shopping and etc. I think ₹40,000 is enough for every indian monthly expenses. Now, We have ₹60,000 left. In ₹60,000 we have put ₹30,000 for emergency funds. Now, We have left ₹30,000 and these ₹30,000 we can invest in somewhere like stocks. So, This is money management.

Let's how we can use it in stock trading. I am going to make you understand with an example.

For example:- The share price of 'XYZ' is ₹400 and we took 10 buy trades in it. Our
stop loss is ₹380 and our take profit is ₹460. It means our loss is ₹20 and profit is ₹60.
Let's assume if we made losses in 6 trades and made profits in 4 trades, So, What do you think we are profitable or not?

Let's calculate it. Our losing trades are 6 and winning trades are 4 and our loss per trade is ₹20 and our profit is ₹60. So, 20 * 6 = ₹120 and 60 * 4 = ₹240. Now, 240 - 120 = ₹120. So, we are still profitable even after losing 6 trades out of 10.

What if we made losses in 7 trades and made profits only in 3 trades. Let's calculate it. 20 * 7 = ₹140 and 60 * 3 = ₹180. Now, 180 - 140 = ₹40. So, We are still in profit.

Money management is a powerful concept to making money in stock trading.

27:) The end words

So, This is the final chapter of this book and if you have read the entire book and understood everything then congratulations.

So, Myself Abdul Wahid Ansari and I am from Rajasthan India. I have been in this field since 2019. I wrote this book just for educating people about this market. I hope, I have done it in the best way.

I did not use long sentences and just tried to make you understand each topic in an easy way and few lines.

If you want to connect with me on social media then here's my Instagram id = wahid_since_02

Thank you
Happy trading

Printed by Libri Plureos GmbH in Hamburg,
Germany